Samuel Ward

Lyrical Recreations

Samuel Ward

Lyrical Recreations

ISBN/EAN: 9783744769907

Printed in Europe, USA, Canada, Australia, Japan

Cover: Foto ©ninafisch / pixelio.de

More available books at **www.hansebooks.com**

LYRICAL RECREATIONS

BY

SAMUEL WARD

*Je vous donne avecque ma foy
Ce qu'il y a de mieulx en moy.*

London
MACMILLAN AND CO.
1883

TO THE EARL OF ROSEBERY,

Decori Scotiæ et Humanitatis.

THE muse I wooed at fifty-two
    Bore me these urchin lays,
Which raise their lowly heads anew
    Since quickened by thy praise.

Will they live on, to vindicate
    The memory of their sire,
Whom Fate compelled to leave to fate
    These foundlings of his lyre?

What care we? Ere the pyramids
    The priests of Isis sang,
While on the kingly coffin-lids
    The graver's chisel rang,

Carving great deeds on stone to cheat
    Oblivion of its prey,
Until the last reveille should beat
    The dawn of Judgment Day.

The priests are dust, the crumbling fane
    In piteous ruin lies;
In loving hearts the holy strain
    Of David never dies.

WHEN in my walks I meet some ruddy lad
   Or swarthy man, with tray-beladen head,
Whose smile entreats me, or his visage sad,
   To buy the images he moulds for bread;

I think that, though his poor Greek Slave in chains,
   His Venus and her Boy with plaster dart,
Be, like the organ-grinder's quavering strains,
   But farthings in the currency of art;

Such coins a kingly effigy still wear,
   Let metals base or precious in them mix;
The painted vellum hallows not the Prayer
   Nor ivory nor gold the Crucifix.

CONTENTS.

	PAGE
To the Earl of Rosebery	v
The Poet's Acre	1
Ignes Fatui	3
Monkhood	5
Time the Auctioneer	11
The Glass-Blower	14
The Monitor	17
Panacea	19
Montauk Light	21
Hymn to Mars	25
The Maiden's Children	28
Ziska	32
Metempsychosis	37
The Wise Maiden	40
The Hebrew Alphabet	42
Porrigo Dextram	44
The Blind Fiddler	47

CONTENTS.

	PAGE
New Music	51
Stradivarius	54
Nocturne	56
Tribute to the Lost Score	59
The Perfect Way	61
The Exile	63
Senescentia	65
Antepenultimate	67
The Morrow of the Funeral	69
The Old Rope	73
Falconry	77
The Charge	85
Lost and Found	86
A Royal Abode	92
Vathek	95
Sub Tegmine Fagi	98
Chant du Départ	101
Poignard or Pills?	103
To Alfred Tennyson	105
To the Poet of Farringford	107
To Lady S. G.	111
To Sibell	113
Impromptu to Mrs. Howe	114
Lines written in a Copy of Omar Khayyám	116
To my Niece Daisy interpreting Liszt	117
To Edgar Allan Poe	120

CONTENTS.

	PAGE
TO WALT WHITMAN	122
IMPROMPTU IN AN ALBUM	125
SIRO DELMONICO	126
FRUITION	131
LEAVES AND STARS	133
OCTOBER LAY	135
SONG OF THE WREN	139
ORCHARD FANTASIA	143
A WAKING DREAM	147
THE INCOMPLETE PICTURE	149
THE TRYST	151
TO CONSUELO	156
NOT WINE ALONE	158
THE RUBY GOBLET	161
BOHEMIAN SONG	166
WALTZ	169
MAZURKA	172
DAWN AT MIDNIGHT	174
THE MOON AND THE BEACON	176
LA CHOCOLATIÈRE	178
DOLORES	180
TITIAN TO STELLA	182
"NO CARDS"	184
A DEPARTING BRIDE	186
LIEBESRUHE	188

CONTENTS.

	PAGE
THE MARINER'S BETROTHED	190
CATECHISM	192
METATHALAMIUM	195
ZAMPITA	197
TODESFRAGE	201
GIVE ME JOY	203
IN FIFTH AVENUE	206
TO A WELL-KNOWN CAMELLIA	210
UNDERGRADUATE	212
IMPROMPTU	214
TO GRACE	216
THE VALLEY-LILY	217
SONG	218
LE MANOIR DE LOCKSLEY	221
AT LAST	226
ENFIN	227
LA SYLPHIDE	230
THE SYLPHIDE	231
À LA COMTESSE IDA	236
MA SAINTE AUX ROSES	238
STANCES À SIBELLE	240
À MA GRACE DARLING	242
À LA PRINCESSE MARGOT	244
À LAURE	246

I.

THE POET'S ACRE.

Down the mountain as I wandered,
And upon the landscape pondered,
    Where, as in a net,
Lordly hedge and stately railing
With the farmer's wooden paling
    Intersecting met,

Compassing the field of azure
Of the lake no rigid measure
    Mapped unequally,—
I bethought me, "Such division
Of the plain is a derision,"
    When my roving eye

Rested on the sexton's barrow
Shrinking near the portal narrow
    Of the churchyard green,

Where fill prince and peasant places
Equal as the chessboard's spaces,
    Hold they pawn or queen.

Still the zig-zag path descending,
Came I to a painter blending,
    On a tinier scale,
Under April's sunshine merry,
Meadow, lake, and cemetery
    Sparkling in the vale.

And with passionate expansion,
Free from envy, I the mansion
    And the cot surveyed,
Coveting nor manor pleasant,
Nor the patches which the peasant
    Vexed with hoe and spade.

Happy, though without an acre,
While supplies the paper-maker
    Sod like this fair page,
Into which, at Fancy's hours,
I transplant the wayside flowers
    Of my pilgrimage.

IGNES FATUI.

A DREAM the limner's waking eyes
    Shall strive to seize,
As vainly as the bark that flies
    Before the breeze ;—

A strain that flutters in the ear
    Yet shuns the throat,
As ceases, when you draw too near,
    The linnet's note ;—

An echo which, within a vale,
    Responds no more
Than a belov'd one, by the gale
    Cast dead ashore ;—

The stations of the stars at noon,
    The silvery wake
Poured by the horn of last night's moon
    Upon the lake ;—

The memory of April's grace
   When trees are bare,
Or of December's frosty face
   When June is fair;—

To strike from air those sparks of bliss,
   In solitude,
Which seemed eternal when your kiss
   Its fellow wooed;—

To ask a friend the boon yourself
   Had freely given,
And find him dearer prizing pelf
   Than love or heaven;—

To toil from dawn till day is old,
   With bleeding hands,
Yet fail to find one grain of gold
   In mocking sands;—

So seem and such the shapes that throng
   Him who pursues—
Endeavouring to entrap in song—
   The wayward Muse.

MONKHOOD.

SEMI-RIGID, half-elastic,
Was the pious, old monastic
    Scheme of life;
When the lenten bread of heaven
With a dash of human leaven
    Aye was rife.

Through dark ages, they kept burning
The forbidden lamps of learning
    In their cells;
As, in Afric's sands, the rover,
With protecting stones, doth cover
    The glad wells.

And, with ecstasy, the stainless
Mother loved they, who, in painless
  Travail, bore
HIM whose birth and crucifixion
Loosed the bonds of our affliction
  Evermore.

Lordly herds, on meadows, thriving
Under vineyards, they, by shriving
  Sinners, got.
Pious hinds their wealth augmented,
And their broad lands tilled, contented
  With their lot.

That the Friars worldly pleasure,
In their lay-days, without measure
  Had enjoyed,
And discovered that the madness
Of the revel's sinful gladness
  Left a void;

Taught them that the peasant's toil,
On the mute but grateful soil
  Is a fate

MONKHOOD.

Happier than his wild ambition,
Who aspires to patrician
    Pomp and state.

And the monk, so old and shabby,
Seemed the image of his Abbey,
    Gray and hoary:
Winter's rudest blasts defying,
With its inward and undying
    Warmth of glory.

Chimed the convent-bell a marriage?
He uncoifed his austere carriage,
    And was mortal,
As with benediction saintly,
Ushered he the fond ones quaintly
    Through hope's portal.

But a sad yet tender riot
Sometimes thrilled his pulse's quiet
    With strange charms,
When the holy-water glistened
On the new-born infant, christened
    In his arms.

MONKHOOD.

And you saw each waxen finger
With unconscious twitchings linger
    Round the boy;
As though yearnings, pent and hidden,
Cried within, for the forbidden
    Human joy.

And his eyes, through fond mists glowing,
Saw the babe in stature growing,
    Till the day
When himself its soul might foster,
And, with creed and *Pater-noster*,
    Point the way.

Like the glass a sigh hath clouded,
Brighter shone his gaze when, crowded
    Near the font,
He beheld God's children pressing,
And bestowed a warmer blessing
    Than his wont.

Called the death-bell's lingering knelling
Prince or peasant from life's dwelling
    To depart?

By those Heaven-sent stewards shriven,
Who the imps of sin had driven
    From his heart,

Each a message, as he kissed him,
Whispered softly and dismissed him
    On glad wing;
Like the bark that carries tidings
From a Viceroy's distant bidings
    To his King.

Fiercely they rebuked the scorner,
Tenderly consoled the mourner
    In his sorrow;
Eyes, all moist to-day with sadness,
Shone serene midst festive gladness
    On the morrow.

Thus abroad, with zeal unending,
Rich and poor alike befriending,
    Lived the Friars;
Vigil, fast, and flagellations
Mortified the world's temptations
    And desires.

And when waxed the poor monk paler,
Until granted him Life's gaoler
    His release,
Earth's sad stewardship resigning,
Homeward flew his spirit, pining,—
    Into peace.

TIME THE AUCTIONEER.

STANDS the clock within the hall,
Like a monk against the wall,
Like a hooded monk with eyes
Owl-like, spectral, solemn, wise,
In whose sockets, moon and sun,
Mimic phase and season run ;
While, beneath the face austere,
  "Going ! Gone ! Going ! Gone !"
Time, the ruthless Auctioneer,
  Sells the moments one by one ;
Moments all too cheaply sold,
Save to Love, for lavished gold,
Save to crime, with dagger bold !
Four and twenty times a day
Step the Morrice-dancers gay,

From their tire-room in the clock,
At the hour's impatient knock;
Wind in courteous rigadoon,
Wind in cadence with the tune,
Vanish with its blithsome strain,
  "Going! Gone! Going! Gone!"
Time his hammer raps again.
  Hark! A groan! Hark! A groan!
Groan for that bright hour just past,
Breathed by one would hold it fast,
For the next shall be his last!

Through the western oriel fall
Sunset glories in the hall.
Thus at eve they ever pour
Rainbowed rapture on the floor.
Now the Virgin's lips are pressed
On yon cherub's sculptured rest,
Now ascends a crimson stain
From the storied window-pane,
Till the light of evening skies
Glimmers in those sleepless eyes.

Drink, poor monk, the lingering rays,
   "Going! Gone! Going! Gone!"
Brief their lustre! Brief thy gaze
   On the sun! Day is done!

Pensive, in the twilight hour,
Sits the maiden in her bower;
Broods the felon in his tower.
One—the noon a bride shall see!
One—at noon shall cease to be!

THE GLASS-BLOWER.

From chaos, with creative hand
And fiery breath and magic wand,
I saw an artizan expand
    And mould a crystal earth,
Where Plain and Hill and Sea and Isle
Were blended in the sunny smile
    That saw our Planet's birth.

Where trees sprang up, whose foliage, dyed
Unfadingly in Summer's pride,
Rude Autumn's withering breath defied,
    And Winter's icy blasts;
And ships, becalmed on wrinkled seas,
Though full their sails, felt not the breeze
    That bent their tapering masts.

A city rose upon the shore
And, on its quay, the stevedore
Awaited to unload and store
    That spell-bound navy's freight;
While on the scaffold felons stood,
Unhanged above the multitude,
    Before the prison gate.

In gardens of ungathered fruit,
Young lovers sat whose tongues were mute,
Nor thrilled its spell the anxious lute
    Within the maiden's hands;
They smiled, in bliss without regret,
As only they who feel not yet
    The altar's silken strands.

And when the adept's task was done,
I saw the boy for whom was spun
That globe, its beauties, one by one,
    With childish ardour greet;
Then clutch it with such eager grip
That mountain, city, tree, and ship
    Fell shivered at his feet;

And thought—when down shall shade his chin,
And Fancy mould a world akin
To that bright Earth, unstain'd by sin,
    The adept's fingers wrought—
He'll clutch and lose it, as a boy,
The bubbles which he saw with joy
    In rainbow meshes caught.

Yet, when his disenchanted eyes
Shall cease to see the mirage rise,
Between him and the desert's skies,
    Above the phantom wave,
He'll halt and kneel and cross his hands,—
Nor long the Simoon's shifting sands
    Will mark the new-made grave.

THE MONITOR.

A MISER joined a funeral train,
    With flinty eye,
And thought, "Yon wretch, whose every vein
I drained till naught was left to gain,
    Did well to die."

He passed the cypress-sentried gate
    With footstep firm;
Nay, lighter trod, because elate
"That his was not the lonely fate
    Of that poor worm."

He stood the yawning grave beside,
    All undismayed,
While Delver and Sacristan vied
Which first the coffin's lid should hide
    With eager spade.

Then, homeward sauntering, he passed
    His father's tomb,
And felt his pulses throbbing fast,
In memory of his joy when last
    He, through its gloom,

Saw glittering the radiant hoard,
    His lifelong lust,
Forgetful that, though now its lord,
He soon must by his sire be stored,
    And waste to dust.

But when, at home, to meet him, stole
    The meek-faced lad
Into whose lap must one day roll
The wealth for which he'd pawned his soul,
    His brow grew sad.

PANACEA.

When skies are gray, and droops my mateless heart
    Within this attic drear,
I wander forth into the restless mart,
    Through labour's busy sphere,
    Or thread the moist and dismal lanes,
    Where poverty reveals its pains.

My wind-swept garret then a palace seems,
    A tropic sun my fire,
My books a mine of bliss, while cheerly steams
    The kettle's soothing choir.
    My toast is made, my tea is brewed
    Once more with smiling gratitude.

So I, comparing mine with sadder stars,
  Thus magnify its light,
Which seems to those encaged by misery's bars
  With happiest lustre bright;
  The lot of captive, drudge, or slave
  Is brighter far, beside the grave,

Than mine, compared with that by them
  deplored,
  Or than the grander fate
Of Crœsus, revelling amidst his hoard,
  A king without a state,—
  Though for his standard taketh he
  The measure of my poverty.

MONTAUK LIGHT.

Latitude 41° 4' 12" *N. Longitude* 71° 51' 54" *W.*

BEFORE the stars appear on high,
I open wide my Cyclops eye,
   Like them unseen by day;
Though, while they roll in distant realms,
My vacant face still guides the helms
   That o'er the waters stray.

The only living things I view,
At times, are cormorant and mew;
   Yet, from my stage-box grand,
I watch the drama of the skies,
And hear, through awful symphonies,
   The Storm-King lead his band.

When clouds obscure the starry host,
My smile beams brighter on the tossed
    And storm-imperilled ships;
While rock-cleft surges shoreward hie,
Like troubled souls whose bodies lie
    Where yon horizon dips.

Then booms the signal-gun its prayer,
And counts with pulse of wild despair
    The moments that remain
To those upon some bark forlore,
Ere from its wreck their souls shall soar
    Beyond the hurricane.

The dawning day uncurtains night
As on a plain where fierce in fight
    At eve men charged and fell;
The slain, amid bale, plank, and spar,
Though undefaced by bruise or scar,
    The Tempest's victory tell,

On serpent waves, that languidly
Unroll their coils along the sea,
    With victims satiate,

Until to sharp resentment urged,
By jutting points of rocks submerged,
    Their dripping jaws dilate.

Yet as to Shakespeare, so to me,
Thaleia and Melpomene
    Alternate come and go;
Once more flits by the merry fleet
Of barks, as in a royal street
    The chariots to and fro.

The full-plumed ship, the wingless car
That, shuttle-like, to strands afar,
    Bears that bright thread of gold
Which weaves, with human sympathy,
Between the warps of sky and sea,
    The New World to the Old.

And I survive the barks that ply
Above the wrecks and crews that lie
    Beneath the glutton wave,
As stately cenotaphs outlive
The mourners who have met to grieve
    Around a new-made grave.

The cross, upon the only fane
That decks some lone and dreary plain,
    Sees not the temples fair
Which, stretching in a zone sublime,
Take up in turn its belfry's chime
    And girt the earth with prayer :

Nor I, adown the seaboard line,
My giant kin with eyes benign,
    On keys and headlands ramp ;
Like pickets posted on the shore,
Where quicksands lurk and breakers roar,
    Before the Atlantic camp.

As when a father shares his gold,
The sun, ere day's last knell is tolled,
    Confides to each a ray,
And like a captain when the word
And pass at change of guard are heard,
    He bids us watch till day.

HYMN TO MARS.

SINCE ages dim in deathless sleep,
As knights in bronze sepulchral keep
    O'er tombs their silent guard,
Thy lone watch thou, with stately pace,
Hast measured in creation's race,—
    Mars with the golden beard!

But brighter glows thy ruddy eye,
When Heav'n's grand minuet brings thee nigh[1]
    To Earth whilom endeared;
And, o'er thy fiery cheek, a smile
Of happy dreams doth play the while,—
    Mars with the golden beard!

[1] Written in June, 1860, when Mars, in his perigee, had shortened his greatest distance from the earth by something more than one hundred and fifty millions of miles.

HYMN TO MARS.

Dreams of thy brief terrestrial home
On Tiber's banks, in infant Rome
   Where thou art still revered;
When Rhea left the vestal shrine
To bear thee Romulus Quirinine,—
   Mars with the golden beard!

Creation's mighty problem solved,
And out of chaos dark evolved
   The star for man prepared,
With thee there came a spirit band,
From higher spheres, to grace the land,—
   Mars with the golden beard!

Like birds in spring on Arctic rocks,
Or mariners, who from ocean's shocks,
   To some lone isle have veered,
Cleaving ethereal realms of light,
Ye landed on Olympus' height,—
   Mars with the golden beard!

They on glad plains, in moulds of grace,
Fashioned and beautified our race;
   In Etna's caverns seared,

HYMN TO MARS.

The sword to Vulcan gavest thou,
From which he forged the primal plough,—
    Mars with the golden beard!

To nature wild abandoned long,
In sportive dance and festive song,
    Earth's children first were reared;
Thy brother Gods loved, drank, and ate,
E'en Zeus himself threw off all state,—
    Mars with the golden beard!

But thou didst teach the sons of toil
To delve the brown glebe's fecund soil
    'Neath flowery meads unspared;
In vernal months to plant and sow,
To harvest when days shorter grow,—
    Mars with the golden beard!

And when, years o'er, their task was done,
From earth rebounding to the sun,
    By man more loved than feared,
Each sought his planet-home afar,
And with them, thou, red God of War,—
    Mars with the golden beard!

THE MAIDEN'S CHILDREN.

Suggested by Miss Stebbins's statue of the Lotus-Eater.

A MAIDEN in her summer bloom,
    Whose heart had neither felt love's thorn
    Nor yet rejected love with scorn,
Lamented thus her sex's doom :—

" Ah me ! whose gaze dare not engage
    In mystic tilt with belted knight,
    Nor venture e'en in sport to plight
A glance to squire or beardless page ;

" Exposed to cold and sordid eyes,
    Like Georgian nymph in Eastern mart,
    Who only may her hand impart
To him whose gold her beauty buys ;

"Whilst—like the incandescent blush,
  That with feigned warmth doth tantalise
  Earth's breast congealed 'neath Arctic skies—
Electric thrills my being flush;

"As though within me gleamed a fire
  Unfed—a glowing, not a burning—
  A coming thirst, a nascent yearning,
A subtle, nameless, vague desire.

"Ah! would my soul from Earth were free;
  For, like the puzzled bird that flies
  'Twixt fowler's net and serpent's eyes,
I dread my sex's destiny!"

An angel heard the maiden's sigh,
  And gently led her spirit where
  In dreams she saw a temple, fair
With chiselled forms not doomed to die:—

The brow of Jove, serene, august;
  The breathing, almost blushing, frame
  Of Psyche, whose ethereal name
The soul takes when it leaves the dust;

Apollo listening to his lyre;
   Minerva softened by its strains;
   And she within whose sea-born veins
For ever burns Love's unquenched fire;

The Graces three, the sacred Nine
   Whose snowy brows and vestal hearts
   Defied the Boy-God's flame-tipped darts;
And mortals more than half divine.

But when the maiden's slumber broke,
   Those god-like shapes, through memory stealing
   And Art's ideal world revealing,
To new resolves her soul awoke.

A roofless shrine deep in the glade,
   Where leant, neglected, moss-bestained,
   The marble god who there had reigned,
Hallowed her vow, with fervour made

On bended knee: "The unwed Bride
   Of Art divine henceforth I'll be;
   And rear a spotless family,
With all a mother's love and pride.

THE MAIDEN'S CHILDREN.

" My travail thus shall realise,
  Without a pang, her chastest joys;
  In snowy marble shall my boys
Beneath my fostering hands arise.

" Since to their frames I may not give
  The quickening pulses of my heart,
  My soul its graces shall impart,
And in their stainless bodies live.

" Their snowy shapes, without defect,
  Angelic beauty shall display;
  No inborn sin of mortal clay
Shall envious eye in them detect."

And as a form embalmed in song
  Awakens to the music sweet
  Which lulled it in its winding-sheet,
So did the maiden's touch, ere long,

Awake to life, with pious art,
  The graceful phantom here congealed;
  A Phœnix, though in snow revealed,
Out of the ashes of her heart.

ZISKA.

WHEN first my infant eyes took in the glory
   Of this fair earth,
Ere on them fell the shadow of the story
   Of mortal birth,
The blessed light above seemed but one fusion
   Of many a sun,
And closing, they imprisoned the illusion
   That Heaven was won.

When I looked forth again, God's bright creation
   Revealed its forms
Beneath the orb which every constellation
   Illumes and warms.

' I then discovered 'mid the heavenly spaces
        Vast depths of blue,
And on the earth the landscape's myriad graces,
        Of varied hue;

Unconscious that, as cleared the golden vision,
        It darker grew,
I revelled in green fields and groves Elysian
        With joys all new;
The sun seemed sent to me alone for reading
        Nature's great book,
O'er which I pored wherever fancy, leading,
        My footsteps took.

Oh, then, Aladdin-like, I gathered treasures
        On golden stems;
First fruits and flowers, then clutched at empty pleasures,
        As precious gems.'
But soon these luresome objects lost their shimmer,
        As in a ball,
When wax-lights wane, the waltzer's eyes flit dimmer
        Around the hall.

To childhood's lively joys succeeded sorrows
   Poignant and stern,
As he who from a miser silver borrows,
   Gold must return;
For manhood hath no sportive recreations
   Like schoolboy plays,
No anguish keener than when in vacations
   Come rainy days.

And soon my soul began its second training
   With new-born zest;
I thought to spend one half of life explaining
   What meant the rest;
And found the problem solved and the equation
   Like some tall peak
Attained, which reaches but the adumbration
   Of what you seek.

And when with every sense alive to Nature,
   By day and night,
Familiarly I knew her every feature
   Shaded and bright;

With adolescence came an empty craving
    For the unknown;
As thinks the spendthrift butterfly of saving
    When summer's gone.

And then, the sad reflection realising,
    How brief is life,
Behold the soul against the senses rising
    In bitter strife.
Existence, like the fleeting year, had seasons,
    And in the end—
I could not through its gloom divine the reasons—
    Must graveward tend.

Through misty tears, a God-like face and lowly
    In rainbows beamed,
Around whose bleeding brow a radiance holy,
    Upshooting, gleamed.
But though toward earth big drops of blood still rolling,
    Did lingering fall,
He said with tender voice, His pain controlling,
    "I died for all."

Since from His bow-shaped lips, like golden arrows
   Those words did speed,
No more my heart an endless craving harrows
   With hunger's need;
Already, when I lift my eyes to heaven,
   I see but light,
And scenes once fair below, from morn to even
   Are dark as night.

METEMPSYCHOSIS.

The God, the Hero, and the Sage,
    Nor sceptre, sword, nor myrtle crown,
    Nor e'en a drop have handed down
Of bubbling blood to this our age.

Caught in the marble or the brass,
    They smile or frown their joy or grief
    From statue, coin, or bas-relief,
Which, though in fashion they surpass

The chiselled thoughts of modern days,
    Bring to our eyes but traits of men,
    Who, like ourselves, on earth have been
The shrines of Life's ephemeral blaze.

But deeds and words embalmed in song,
  In after ages—like the seed
  From royal mummies drawn to feed
The tribes which Egypt's river throng—

Dilate fresh hearts and sublimate
  The lowliest blood with flames heroic,
  And fortify with valour stoic
The weak against the storms of fate.

Yes, as the shivered chord's complaint
  Floats onward through the murmuring air,
  Until some unison as fair
Responds into its whisper faint,—

So, when it severs earth's last thread,
  The soul pursues its journeying,
  And swells, on fleet and tireless wing,
The shadowy army of the dead;

Until it chance a kindred chord
  Within some brother's sleeping heart
  To wake, and its own life impart
To sage's lips or warrior's sword.

METEMPSYCHOSIS.

Napoleon fought with Caesar's blade,
   Dante was god-like Homer's son,
   Timoleon prompted Washington,
And Paul stout Luther's fierce crusade.

Nor in such mighty souls alone
   Do kindred spirits breathe their fire;
   The humblest heart's untutored lyre
From shadowy voices takes its tone.

Until they sound, bend every string
   Thy hand can grasp, with zealous care,
   Though from thy lyre but hoarse despair
Fate's ruthless sweep at first should wring.

Strain on! until thy spirit's Sire
   Awake that chord of happier fate,
   Whose jubilance shall modulate
Thy woe to joy's celestial choir.

TO MY DAUGHTER,
MRS. MARGARET ASTOR CHANLER.

THE WISE MAIDEN.

MASTER.

PRITHEE, why for ever sweeping,
    Maiden, this poor room?
Ever stirring, never sleeping,
    Seems thy restless broom.

Prithee, why for ever praying,
    Those pure lips within?
Art, I fear, too dearly paying
    For but fancied sin.

THE WISE MAIDEN.

MAID.

Though I'm ever sweeping, master,
    Did my zeal grow slack,
Than it disappeareth faster
    Would the dust come back;

And my praying is but sweeping
    This poor sinful breast,
Into which fresh dust is creeping,
    When from prayer I rest.

MASTER.

Never does my eye remember,
    Maiden, to have seen,
When thy care hath swept my chamber,
    Speck of dust within.

MAID.

May the angel to my sweeping
    Praise like this impart,
Who, his master's mansions keeping,
    Comes to search my heart.

אדני

THE HEBREW ALPHABET.

Come, my little Hebrew lad,
On thy task look not so sad.
Only learn it, and thou'lt feel
Writing is in prayer to kneel;
Writing, in His sacred tongue,
Words His holy prophets sung;
Writing out the law bequeathed
Unto Moses, when He breathed,
Near the burning bush, the Word
Then as now, "I am the Lord."
First we'll learn to spell the name
Sinai heard in clouds and flame.
Write the *Aleph*—every sign
Let thy pen with love design.

THE HEBREW ALPHABET.

Aleph is bright Eden's token,
Ere our race by sin was broken.
Daleth follows in the spell
Loved in Heaven, feared in Hell.
Aleph, Daleth, lowly now
On our bended knees we bow,
Ere unto the Holy Rune
We append the closing *Nun*.
Adon Adon, clap your hands,
Hills! while joy elates the lands;
Once more write, and with a *Yod*,
Tremble at the name of God!
God with whom none others vie,
God of Israel! 𝔄𝔡𝔬𝔫𝔞𝔦.

אדני

PORRIGO DEXTRAM.

WHILE sorrows ebb and flow
    On Life's gray strand,
To all oppressed by woe
    I reach a hand.

The body's but a cell,
    Its jailer he
Whose key from earth's dark spell
    Shall set us free.

Stars, though unseen by day,
    Still glow in wells,
Where truth's unwelcome ray
    In exile dwells.

Like barks, wave-tossed till sore,
    Upon the deep,
Within our souls a store
    Of wealth we keep.

Then, brother, here's my hand,
    Though void its palm,
Beside thee will I stand
    Till God send balm;

Beside thee float, while hold
    Two planks together,
Till melts His sun this cold
    And wintry weather.

When that ray shines, we part,
    But thou shalt stay;
Another sinking heart
    Calls me away.

And should hope's dawning beams
    To gems congeal,
Bright as the diamond stream
    Of Maund reveal,

Swear that a brother's cry,
By sea or land,
Shall ever draw thee nigh
With helping hand.

THE BLIND FIDDLER.

Who knocks?   Come in !   Thy message say.
A beggar?   Sixpence—go thy way !
A fiddler too ?   A shilling take
And go ; nor dare my nerves to shake.
Thy little handmaid says thou'rt blind,
Each eye, a sixpence more.   That's kind.
Two shillings not enough?   Ingrate !
Well, let the little maiden prate.
"Please, sir, his poor old viol's strung ;
For thanks he has no other tongue."
A tear?   "Its strings he fain would sweep,
Few thank when they a harvest reap."
Well, play, old man.—That timid air
Steals through me like an infant-prayer.
Now swells the bow to fuller strains
Exhaling riper joys and pains

Of youth and manhood,—old man, stay
Thy fingers! picture not decay,
But Love, the Dance, the Festal Song,
The Squadron's Charge, the Altar's Throng.
Here, take my purse—my blessing too,
Thou'st shown me something yet to do.

And when thou'rt gone, I'll hie me forth,
Convinced there still are joys on earth,
Though not the passions, pride and power,
Which wither in life's sunset-hour ;
But Nature's every charm and grace—
For ages wrinkle not her face—
A steadfast Love, to Friendship kin,
The victory of soul o'er sin ;
And charities, like cargoes sent
To distant climes, which tenfold rent
Bring back to hearts whose happy glow
Is fed by what themselves bestow.
And all these fragrant flowers hath twined
About my heart a fiddler blind !

The poet hath no keener sight
Than this old man with vision blight,

Who, piercing with the spirit's eye
The veil of his infirmity,
Hath with his viol's quickening spell
My pinions warmed to break their shell;
If I accomplish half the task
He wrought on me—'t is all I ask.

DIALOGUE.

POET.

Round my heart thy viol flings
Rapture, with four magic strings.
If thy bow, with but the spell
Of twelve semitones, can tell,
Like the rod that gold divines,
All the ear's unfathomed mines,
Spells how many wields the pen,
To delight the hearts of men?

FIDDLER.

Countless as the shore's gray sands
Are the spells the pen commands;

Earth, and they who on it dwell,
Space and Ocean, Heaven and Hell.
Be thy soul with these chords strung
Fervently, and pen and tongue,
Thrilling deeper, hearts shall raise
Higher than my lowly lays.

POET.

By the measure thou hast taught
I will sell what life hath bought,
I will give thy song a shape,
Ere its fleeting tones escape.

FIDDLER.

Mock thou not my humble art!
With my bow, God touched thy heart,
And to Him ascend its strains,
While thy song on earth remains.

NEW MUSIC.

When sounds an air that thrills your ears
With memories of bygone years,
Forgetting age and care and pain,
The soul puts on its youth again;
And she who shone in beauty's pride,
Long faded, sparkles at your side;
And as in spring old wines ferment
When buds and leaves on vines are blent,
So through your quickened pulses pour
The effervescent joys of yore.
Again her name drops from your lip
Into the brimming cup you sip;
Nay, in the amber wine you trace
The image of her cherished face.
O days of youth and wild delight!
O gladdening waters, sweet as bright,

Which memory's melodious spells
Uncover like the desert's wells!

Another sits in gloom and pain
Whilst you drink in the rapturous strain.
As East winds open ancient wounds,
His bleed afresh at those sweet sounds;
It is the air, that lured him on
To wretchedness in days bygone,
Which now relumes the witching gaze
Of those dark eyes whose treacherous rays
To ashes burnt his youth so fair,
And left his life one long despair,
Renewed, as with those notes arise
His heart's burnt-offerings to the skies,
And leave it, when the strains expire,
An altar blackened by the fire.
The sun grows pale, the air is chill,
Grim skeletons his vision fill;
In death no greater terrors lie,
For thus to suffer is to die.

Now, like fond brothers, hand in hand,
Both tread some fair and unknown strand,

In measure; when the magic wand
Of SCHUMANN sways the tuneful band,
Or WAGNER'S glorious voices smite
The ear, and unsipped joys unlock,
As when the patriarch Israelite
With faith-borne rod struck Horeb's rock.

One, wafted to the fairy isle
On ocean's softest summer smile;
One, 'scaped with life and nothing more
From ocean's fiercest wintry roar:
Both drink its odours, breeze-beguiled
From thicket and savanna wild;
Both taste its tropic fruitage filled
With sweetness from the sun distilled:
Both bask in blooms that never change
From sea-side up to mountain range;
Till to their ravished senses seem
Life's bliss and bale an equal dream,
And each, in ecstasy, forgets
The past—its joys and its regrets.

STRADIVARIUS.

When the viol hath been strung,
And the master's hand hath wrung
Speech from every hermit tongue
    That unseen dwells
    Within its cells;
Hoarse its voices until taught
With its rapture to consort,
Or, in sweet concent, to show
Sympathy with human woe.

Then, in their retiredness,
Craving constantly to bless
Air and ear with tuneful stress,
    Each mellower grows
    In its repose,

Till a fuller choral swell,
And a softer waning spell,
Are the echoes that respond
To the master's magic wand.

When the viol's tones aspire
Upward, like the breath of fire,
Does the master's soul inspire
    Alone its sighs
    And symphonies?
Or do angels with the strain
Seek their long-lost home again,
Soaring in melodious throng
On the pinions of his song?

When a friend hath ceased to groan,
While we o'er his coffin moan,
And deplore his spirit flown,
    Dare we maintain
    That ne'er again
Shall that unstrung harp be wound
And the Master's glory sound?
May not, then, the lute enshrine
Unseen spirits half divine?

NOCTURNE.

MAIDEN, while thy fairy fingers
Free those prisoned harmonies,
While thy left hand softly lingers,
And thy right skims o'er the keys,
Darting as hussars manœuvre,
Skirmishing in mazy drill,
Swift to scatter, and recover
Order at their leader's will;

Dreamily I hear two voices,
One in fervent tones of prayer,
One that sparkles and rejoices
As a skylark in the air,
With so wild a jubilation
That its carol seems a taunt,
Till a sterner modulation
Drops it to the dominant.

NOCTURNE.

Then a dialogue more tender
'Twixt the wooer and the wooed,
Where the latter vows to mend her
Wayward petulance of mood ;
And the manly voice responding
Breathes a rapture of content,
As through chords with joy resounding
Both in unison are blent.

Through the moonlit fir-trees playing,
Murmuringly the roving breeze
Kisses the white fingers swaying
Pensively the ivory keys,
Cools my brow and soothes the beating
Of this scarred and crippled heart,
Still, despite experience, cheating
Me with fond delusive art.

Cheating me with phantoms thronging
Dimly up from days of yore,
Shapes of loveliness and longing
Dead and gone for evermore.

And as wizards from the ashes
Of the rose evoke its grace,
I recall the spectral flashes
Of a once all-radiant face.

TRIBUTE TO THE LOST SCORE.

*To a young friend lamenting the loss
of her teens.*

YEARS are but the tools of youth,
Spades that turn the sod of Truth,
Symbols on a black-board traced,—
Traced in chalk to be effaced,—
Scaffoldings to rear and prop
Work the seasons cannot stop.
For, though marmots hybernate,
Man's live pulses never bate,
Nor lie fallow like the field
Resting from its autumn yield.
So until we reach the brink,
We must either grow or shrink.

TRIBUTE TO THE LOST SCORE.

Years are tomes the student lone,
Poring over, makes his own;
Or the fruits, Earth, Sun, and Air
Quicken for his destined fare,
Like the ship that bears us o'er
Safely to a distant shore,
Or the ducats that we spend
To attain a journey's end.
So the years that make us men,
Aye, or women, are a gain;
Strength to fight or grace to win,
Prove what friends those years have been.

Maiden, though Time's ruthless shears
From thy life lop twenty years,
For the lost score only grieve
Thou hast twenty less to live.
Those have left a crystalline
Charm upon thy face benign;
Spirit-beauty, virtue, grace,
Time may envy, not deface;
Scythe and glass, his emblems gaunt,
Fail to scratch the adamant.

THE PERFECT WAY.

Lines sent with a book bearing the above title.

THE Perfect Way—ah, who shall say
   He holds the mystic clue,
Up that steep rath the hidden path
   To find and to pursue?

No stars above with eyes of love
   Direct us when astray;
With faith and hope we feel and grope
   Through thick'ning gloom our way.

Anon around sweet voices sound,
   And breaths of frankincense,
As breezes thrill a glassy rill,
   Awake each latent sense.

To climb and pant, the Hierophant
    The Acolyte hath doomed,
Until within the dross of sin
    By penance be consumed.

Then sorely tried and mortified,
    The flesh to spirit yields,
With truer might than in the fight
    The hero's sabre wields.

THE EXILE.

THEY who in the churchyard sleep,
Or the bosom of the deep,
Or beneath the sabre's sweep,
    Are not all that die;
Other loved ones pass away,
Whom we mourn as dead, while they
    With the living hie.

Homeward turns the funeral train;
"Brother! freed from mortal pain,
Thou in warmth wilt rise again
    From thy cold repose;
When the sea its dead shall yield,
And the gorgéd battle-field
    Shall its lips unclose."

Time dries tears ; and jest and laugh
Crown the brimming cup we quaff,
Long before his epitaph
    Moss and age efface ;
Nay, the shipwreck's fearful story,
Or the combat's victims gory,
    Years from memory chase.

But when boyhood's melodies
Shed their dew in festive eyes,
Through soft mists we see arise
    Phantom-like, the friend,
Dead, yet living, who from home,
Is in exile doomed to roam
    To life's dreary end.

SENESCENTIA.

In my youthful hey-day, pleasure
    Lured me to its glad unrest,
And the goblet's mantling measure
    Fed the joy-flames in my breast;
Life was rapturous commotion
    Then of body, heart, and mind,
I, a bark upon the ocean,
    Pressed by wave and kissed by wind.

But the sailor quits the fountains
    Of the ever-throbbing main,
Gladly for the steadfast mountains
    And the stillness of the plain,
Wave and wind at length together
    Strain the seams and cords of life,
While on land in mildest weather
    Rooted we abide the strife.

So I fled the blood's temptation
    As the mariner the seas,
Fanned thenceforth to contemplation
    Only by the living breeze;
Onward since serenely treading,
    Yielding now to reason's sway,
Now the paths of fancy threading
    I am master of my way.

All my being now is yearning
    For the rapture of repose,
Youthful flame and manhood's burning
    Quenched like torches dipped in snows;
Every siren's charms transcending
    Blessed be the angel, who
Thus prepares my soul for wending
    The Nirvâna's portals through.

ANTEPENULTIMATE.

Shall I sit and wait for Death,
With a sigh at every breath
For the hours of gladness flown,
From the present drear and lone?
Sit, abandoning all hope
Of a brighter horoscope?
Sit, as in a skiff that glides
Down some rapid's angry tides?
Sit, nor dash a valiant oar
To regain the rugged shore?
Yes! I'm weary of the fight;
Ajax-like, my smitten sight
Findeth neither in the day
Nor the night, a cheering ray;
Though the shore by which I glide
Is my native river-side,

And the hamlets that arise
Wear the old familiar guise ;
Though yon steeple points the road
Pious forefathers have trod.

In the church, another voice
Bids the kneeling fold rejoice ;
In the hall another squire
Sits before the yule-log fire ;
All are strangers,—why should I
'Midst them tarry, but to die?

THE MORROW OF THE FUNERAL.

My room is dark—but darker yet
    The cell where he lies low
For whom our eyelids still are wet,
    Our hearts still throb with woe.

My room is cold—the Western breeze,
    That wakes me with its breath,
Above him stirs the aspen trees,
    But not his sleep of death.

Just now I dreamed that sweet and fair
    I saw his kindly face;
He dreams no more: he waits us where
    Nor death nor dream hath place.

Yes ! ours the darkness, his the light ;
   I clasp his outstretched hand
Whose feet have found, through doubt and
    night,
   The sure and shining land.

II.

THE OLD ROPE.

"FATHER! what is this old rope?"
Boy! 'twas once our vessel's hope
   When the billows rose in rage her decks
     to whelm;
In that wild September gale,
Which had rent our every sail,
   With that bit of rope I lashed her helm.

Had its strands then given way,
We had been the fishes' prey,
   At their banquet in the sea's deep caves;
But I never lost my grip
Of that rope which held the ship
   Till the winds had made peace with the
     waves.

THE OLD ROPE.

How the mariner exults,
When he feels the throbbing pulse
   Of the ocean lashed to fever by the gale,
And his hand directs the course
Of his vessel, like a horse
   Madly tearing over hill and over dale !

Ah ! the boldest charioteer
Were beside himself with fear,
   If a steed in his teeth the bit should take,
Not on solid hill or plain,
But across the slippery main,
   Where the path writhes beneath him like a snake.

There be those that gather nests
Down the Orkneys' sea-girt crests,
   Who are lowered by a rope like this,
And who, when their scrips are full,
Give the signal-cords a pull,
   To be hoisted up out of the abyss.

Yet the boldest ne'er dissemble
How much now and then they tremble,

THE OLD ROPE.

When they feel their lives hang on such
    a bight,
Though those fowlers, when they climb,
Risk but one life at a time,
    While this rope held a score of us that
    night.

But no feeble hand of man
Thus from parting kept its span,
    And our vessel from the trough of the sea;
It was God who held it there,
For I breathed a breath of prayer,
    Like the fishers on the lake of Galilee.

When I'm summoned by the Lord,
Round my coffin let this cord
    Drop me like a fowler seeking for a nest;
And another boon I crave
Is that by me, in the grave,
    This old and trusty friend of mine shall rest.

Dare an unbeliever say
That on Resurrection Day,

It may not serve to raise me from the
 grave?
Like the fowler with his scrip,
Or our storm-imperilled ship,
 Which its strands from destruction helped
 to save?

TO JULIA ROMANA HOWE.

FALCONRY.

Sorcerer.

" If to avert, O king,
    The doom of death at morn,
My voice had summoned thee,
    I should deserve thy scorn.

" To save my worthless life
    These lips shall frame no prayer
Nor ask a boon of thee;
    But if thy daughter fair,

" What time the noose shall bind
    My throat at break of day
Will smile upon me from
    Yon lattice o'er the way;

" And round her snowy neck
    The lilac sash will wear
Which girt her waist that eve
    My hand was torn from there;

" And let its waving bands,
    Which fell below her knee,
Appear to hold her looped
    As will the halter me;

" And last, if when I drop
    Her head shall sink beneath
The casement-sill, as though
    Resolved to share my death;—

" Pledge this, and ask what boon
    A wizard may impart,—'
A spark to fire thy veins,
    A hoard to freeze thy heart."

KING.

" All this and more I grant,—
    Thy life and her white hand,

The sceptre and the crown
   By which I rule the land,

" Whereof thou shalt be king,
   And I will go my ways,—
If thou'lt impart the spell
   Of never-ending days."

Sorcerer.

" The kneeling boor, whose shoulder
   Is smitten by thy sword,
Arises, by the spell
   Of kingly words a lord.

" But whom my wand shall touch,
   Be high or low his birth,
My whispered charm can make
   The richest of the earth.

" The Shibboleth of life
   Would lose my soul, if told ;
For what I ask, be thine
   The charm of endless gold."

KING.

" So thou wilt prove that spell
    Upon the chains that hold
Thy body, and transmute
    Their iron into gold ;

" My daughter from yon lattice
    Shall smile on thee, nor falter
When in the morn the hangman
    Shall loop thee with the halter ;

" The lilac sash she wore,
    The night I found thy grasp
Around her in the garden,
    Her snowy neck shall clasp :

" And on the lattice bow
    Its waving ends I'll tie,
That she may seem to thee
    Like thee about to die ;

" And when beneath thy feet
    The fatal bolt is sped,

I swear that she shall bend,
  Saluting thee, her head."

Sorcerer.

" Now cross yon hazel wand
  Upon thy royal sword,
And swear by Him who died
  That thou wilt keep thy word.

" 'Tis well—dismiss these slaves,
  Now take the hazel wand:
The serpent-head in thine,
  The tail in my right hand.

" Thine ear bring close and listen,
  And after me recite
The measured incantation,
  And grasp the hazel tight.

" Nay, open not thine eyes
  So wide, as in dismay;
No coward will the Gnome
  Who guards the mine obey.

"The Sprite must know a master
    Or else the master he:
The second rune is faster;
    Repeat it after me.

"Thy face is pale, O monarch,
    And all alive thy hair;
Pause not! or of the malice
    Of Gnome and Sprite beware.

   .   .   .   .   .

"'Tis said—now touch my chains,
    Ha! they grow yellow straight,
And from my wrists I feel
    Them hang with heavier weight

"Now get the charm by rote;
    A word misplaced rebounds
As from a rock the ball
    Which him who shot it wounds.

"Ah, so! these chains thou fain
    Wouldst in the furnace try?

Exchange them—and thou'lt find
  Their gold no jugglery."

At dawn beneath the gibbet
  Serene the wizard stood,
And saw within the lattice
  The princess he had wooed.

Around her neck the sash
  As round his throat the cord;
Then knew he that the king
  Had kept his royal word.

For, by its fastened ends,
  The lilac noose was hung,
As from the gallows-tree
  The rope that held him swung.

And when their glances met,
  Upon her lip and eye
He saw a radiant smile,
  And said—"Now let me die."

And when the trap was sprung,
  The princess dipped her head;

But when they came to raise her,
  They found her spirit fled ;

And 'twixt those corpses twain,
  They saw a falcon bear
Aloft, with clenchéd talons,
  A white dove through the air.

THE CHARGE.

CANTER on, canter on, gaily we go !
Let no betrayal our trumpeters blow,
Till we behold on yon summit the foe
    Loose not the bugle's wild breath ;
Then to its sound we will bound o'er the ground,
    Jubilant unto the death.

Tighten your girths as we rise yonder slant,
Slacken your pace, let your weary steeds pant,
Hark ! 'tis the enemy's rude battle-chant,—
    Grow to your saddles, my men !
We're on the hill—blow your will, bugles shrill !
    Now for a crash in the glen !

LOST AND FOUND.

I.

LOST.

*To Major C * * *, U. S. Infantry, reported
"dead on the field of honour" at Gaines's Mill,
June 27th, 1862.*

A LEGEND of the guillotine,
   Or of the gibbet's vengeful cord,
Or of two foes at sunrise seen
   To grasp the pistol or the sword,—
May for a beat our pulses stop,
   While fancy sees the axe descend,

LOST AND FOUND.

The pinioned felon hopeless drop,
    The slayer o'er his victim bend.

When one, of old a comrade, dies,
    His life-march flits before our ken,
Dim passing shadows that arise
    Upon a wall, to fall again;
But being told some dearer brow
    Lies cold 'neath Azrael's marble seal,
As to a cannon-shot we bow,
    And nearer to the graveyard feel.

But fancy's self-adjusted glass
    May not include the vaster woe
Of crews that storm-fiends, as they pass,
    In ocean's barren furrows sow :
Or of gay legions, which with pride
    Of crested ranks clothed hill and dale,
Swept down by battle's furious tide,
    Like stately grain by summer's hail.

'Twas thus on me this strife had gleamed
    But as an airy pageant's show

Of war's bold game, which well beseemed
    Its varying chances' ebb and flow;
Until it like a mirage waned
    And bared thy mortal wound—O friend,
With whom the parting toast I drained
    Was, " May the conflict quickly end ! "

The Old Year sank within our bowl,
    And when the New in splendour rose,
I should have wept—heroic soul !—
    To think thou wouldst not see its close;
To dream that Atropos then held,
    E'en then, the scissors near thy thread,
And that our goblet-chimes but knelled
    Thy fate, to DEATH AND GLORY wed.

When I recall thy pensive face,
    The smile that smoothed its furrows deep,
The sternness veiled by tender grace,
    As lilies screen a lion's sleep;
I feel that we who weep thee are
    Poor trimmers, who—as sailors guide

Their vessels—waste our souls in care
    To follow, not to breast the tide.

A teacher of the art heroic,
    Who precept with example twines,
Nor counterfeits a virtue stoic
    Against whose rule his soul repines,
Is he who drills a nation's youth
    The call of duty to obey,
To fight the fight of right and truth,
    To point—and more, to lead the way.

Such wert thou, Friend, whose loss I mourn
    As martial seed! Thy fertile yield
Might, like the future's garnered corn,
    Have bearded many a battle-field.
Thy country was thy only wife,
    Thy troop thy only family;
For her thou hast laid down thy life,
    Whose sons had gladly died for thee!

II.

FOUND.

*To Major C * * *, U. S. Infantry, dangerously wounded and made a prisoner at Gaines's Mill, June 27th, 1862.*

My tears fell on an empty grave,
   Yet let them not be shed in vain,
But dedicated to the brave
   Whom thousands mourn amongst the slain.

My dirge, in feeble numbers wrought
   With pious heart, shall consecrate
Their memory whose death has brought
   Such grief as thy imagined fate.

Could tears wake them to life again,
   Their forms heroic would arise,
Like trampled grass from quickening rain,
   Beneath a nation's weeping eyes.

Could plaint or song their ears but thrill
    As thine awoke to hear my strain,
No pen were dry, no voice were still,
    From where they lie to distant Maine.

Yet deem not that my heart retracts
    The praise ne'er meant to dim the eye
Of one whose future words and acts
    Shall verify that eulogy.

I greet thee as some vessel fair
    Her owner hath deplored as lost,
When on his gaze, through summer-air,
    Her white sails glisten off the coast;

And up the cliffs glad neighbours rush,
    With kindred joy, and grasp his hand
Whose moistened cheek the breezes flush
    That waft his lost bark to the land.

A ROYAL ABODE.

If to dwell within a palace,
Out of reach of want or malice,
  Is a king to be;
If the loftier one's storey,
Higher soars one's earthly glory,
  Few are kings like me.

Though a monarch I've no nation
To preserve from grim starvation,—
  I no uproar fear;
But throughout my city stately
Suffered am to walk sedately,
  Free from scowl or sneer.

Me surround no courtiers pettish,
With their capers etiquettish,
  Ceremonious, cold;

A ROYAL ABODE.

Jealous heart-burns ill concealing,
None, because the other, kneeling,
    Doth my slippers hold.

Mine's a life of royal pleasure;
All my days are days of leisure,
    All the nights the same;
When I take an extra bottle,
Cares my throat-latch never throttle,
    No one cries out "Shame!"

And the visions of my slumber
Haggard faces ne'er encumber;
    At my will I rise,
And whene'er it suits my fancy,
Rolls and coffee brings up Nancy
    With the dark-blue eyes.

From my larder's tempting plenty,
Dine alone or dine with twenty
    Or a hundred guests;
Sit till our convivial laughter
Shakes the glasses, thrills the rafter,
    Mingling songs and jests.

Servants many round the table;
Many grooms within the stable;
 Nay, a commodore,
With his word and gesture serious,
On the quarter-deck imperious,
 Is not worshipped more.

Of all this the glad fruition
Hold I upon one condition,
 Sometimes hard to fill—
Hard as chancellor must drudge it
When compelled to shape his budget,—
 I MUST PAY MY BILL.

VATHEK.

My eyes are dim, my thin locks gray,
    The avalanche of years hath bent
My frame—will it suspend decay
    If at your bidding I repent?

Repent! Do monarchs abdicate
    When senses wane and pleasures cloy?
Doth avarice expropriate
    The wealth which buys no other joy?

The hoary king retains his throne,
    The miser's palsied grasp his hoard;
Shall I the crumbling fane disown
    Of which my will is still the lord?

Repent! While Love's bright galaxies
  Still glisten in the blue of sleep,
And shapes once worshipped greet my eyes
  When up the slope I turn to peep?

Read in yon bark that quits the shore,
  The tale, by years and tempests told,
Of planks, without their sap of yore,
  Wave-twisted from the builder's mould.

Yet, while she floats, intrepid tars
  Confide their all to her, nor pause
To think how frail the screen that bars
  Them from the ocean's myriad jaws.

She hath her legends of rare freights,
  Of food to starving peoples borne,
Of silks and teas from China's gates,
  And spices from the Isles of Morn.

When weary of such yarns her crew
  Cast webs, like spiders, to the shore;
Their watch, in tempests, they fight through,
  Then sleep as though the fight were o'er.

If they beyond such hourly care
    Look not, whose cares may cease to-morrow,
Shall I that drift I know not where
    Weigh down my sinking years with sorrow?

The wind is rising; let me glean,
    From Time's heaped sands, such golden grains
As miners gather up between
    The walls of long-exhausted veins.

TO SAMUEL L. M. BARLOW.

SUB TEGMINE FAGI.

You marvel I should bid farewell
    To cities and to men—
At fifty—and contented dwell
    Within this lonely glen.

Long be it ere afflictions give
    Your undimmed faith the lie,
And teach you it is hard to live
    Where those you cherish die!

While here I draw, with every breath,
    Of life a balmy share,
Your city seems the haunt of death
    When to it I repair.

SUB TEGMINE FAGI.

So many of its palaces
    Are sepulchres for me,
Of those who shared a happiness
    That never more shall be;

That when my footsteps pause beside
    Some old friend's dwelling-place,
A gravestone seems the door, once wide
    With welcoming embrace.

And e'en the living few, of al
    My comrades I yet meet,
Seem tottering to a funeral,
    Along the callous street.

Afar from walls in mourning hung,
    And mutes so nigh the tomb,
These forests seem forever young,
    These fields dispel my gloom.

I cannot tell the birds apart
    Which in my beeches sing,
From those which last year taught my heart
    To beat in tune with Spring.

The self-same squirrel seems to trip
　From branch to branch in glee,
That I beheld last summer skip
　About the self-same tree.

The night-hawks, at the close of day,
　The owl to supper call;
The cricket chirps his roundelay
　Beneath my chimney-wall;

And this is why I bade farewell
　To cities and to men—
At fifty—and contented dwell
　Within this lonely glen.

CHANT DU DÉPART.

IN buoyant youth we sing and dance,
    Later we only sing,
Then fade the rainbows of romance,
    Our cymbals cease to ring;
And we, like the enchanted Prince
    All petrified below,
Lament the bright years vanished since
    We tripped with nimble toe.

With kindred fancies, lovely friend,
    So soon to brave the sea,
This minuet of the brain I send,
    Too grave, I fear, for thee.
Alas! too old for dance or song
    My feet and head repose,
But, sweet, my heart still beating strong
    For thee with rapture glows.

And if there be a blissful land
    Where friends hereafter meet,
I'll hail thee there, with beckoning hand,
    On gaily bounding feet.
And in thine ear breathe couplets fair
    To Gabriel's tuneful sway,
And both rejoice that we have there
    No washing-bills to pay!

STEAMSHIP "BRAUNSCHWEIG,"
BALTIMORE, *July* 1875.

POIGNARD OR PILLS?

Margaret of Burgundy,
  Frailest of the frail,
Tempted many a gallant
  To the Tour de Nesle.

With caresses burning,
  Made his soul her own;
Then she softly stabbed him
  Dead—without a groan.

Stabbed him, while her kisses
  Drained his parting breath;
What a modulation
  That—from Love to Death.

Mozart the magician,
  Thus from jubilee
Deftly shifts the tonic
  To a minor key.

As at Juan's banquet,
  Wassail, mirth, and glory,
Freeze to awe when raps
  Il Commendatore,

At each rap a blast
  From the horns of hell,—
No such warning had they
  At the Tour de Nesle.

Were not death more welcome
  —Last of mortal ills—
In a shower of kisses
  Than—a box of pills?

TO ALFRED TENNYSON.

A CURATE in a lonely hamlet preaching,
    Nor heard beyond,
Until with rumours of his saintly teaching
    Echoes respond,
And then into a broader field translated
    With ampler fold,
As soldiers are to higher grades elated
    For actions bold—
Cries, when he hears assembled hundreds voicing
    Responsive prayer,
Hosanna! in yet bolder strains rejoicing
    The distant air.
So thou, in humbler days, didst hymn a wailing
    For Claribel,
Which on the outer world like unavailing
    Entreaty fell;

But friends around thee shared thy tuneful
>weeping,
>>And treasured long
The memory of that hapless maiden sleeping
>>Within thy song.
I see thee now in Art's great temple throning,
>>A Hierophant,
And hear glad voices from far peaks intoning
>>Thy larger chant.

TO THE POET OF FARRINGFORD.

A FRIEND,[1] who in the South now waits
   Until the Sesame
Of peace shall cleave his prison-gates,
   Thus spake to me of thee:

" He dwells in Britain's fairest isle,
   Within an ivy-kirtled pile,
     Gray as its Saxon age;
   Mid flower-brocaded turfs that lie
   On chalk-cliffs, like the minstrelsy
     That broidereth his page.

" He dwells afar from Caerleon
   Where Arthur's dawning glories shone,

---

[1] My friend William Henry Hurlbert, at that time imprisoned at Richmond, expiating his defence of human liberty by the loss of his own.

Nor near to Camelot;
Though in his walks, the spectral throng
Of Paladins applaud his song,
    While weeps Sir Launcelot.

" 'Twas there I heard his silver voice,
In spells his pen had cast, rejoice,
    And saw its tones evoke
The calm procession of his *Dream
Of Women Fair*, until the stream
    Of song by night was broke.

" Next day at even's favouring tide
I left the Isle; and by his side,
    To speed the parting guest,
Stood she, who held in either hand
A flaxen child with golden band
    Clasped round a crimson vest.

" As on them burned day's orange glow,
My fancy pictured Ivanhoe,
    When love had crowned his joys;
Rowena in the bloom of life,
The mother, still with beauty rife,
    Of his two Saxon boys."

Moss-rose Pendennis, when he cast
His petals on our Northern blast,
    To scent its wintry breath,
Swore thou alone of living men,
Within his widely-reaching ken,
    Would'st long survive thy death.

Another came, whose sparkling glow
Might vie with the inspiring flow
    Of Rhone or fairy Rhine,
And vowed thou wert no anchorite,
For once he saw thee half the night
    The cup with garlands twine.

Two portraits of thee near me lie :
In rapture on the Eastern sky
    The younger seems to gaze ;
The other of the Western sun
In autumn, ere the day is done,
    Reflects the saddening rays.

But not thy living fame nor face,
Though tongue or bust their image trace,

Before my soul arise;
I see thee as in after days
Posterity shall with his lays
The minstrel canonize.

TO LADY S. G.

With a White Carnation.

THE pale carnation represents
    A spirit pure,
A soul from every blush of sense
    Henceforth secure.

I see thee in such raiment gleaming
    When, at its edge,
The altar heard thy voice redeeming
    Thy sponsor's pledge.

And next I hear the organ pealing
    Its shout of pride,
When thou, before that altar kneeling,
    Becam'st a bride.

How of such memories the flood
    Can I impart,
While that carnation's primal blood
    Invades my heart?

TO SIBELL.

THE martial pageant that absorbed our gaze
And fired my pulses, when the gladdened air
Quickened with joy the sun's majestic rays,
All disappeared! All save thy face so fair,
Which seemed to say, "A desert at the best
Is life, o'er which the floating mirage-gleams
Incite our paces, until we find rest
Beside some angel of our better dreams."

DOVER HOUSE, *May* 28, 1883.

IMPROMPTU.

To my Sister, Mrs. Julia Ward Howe, on her 54th Birthday.

SIX times nine make fifty-four!
May you live years many more,
Dearest, bravest sister mine
I have loved years six times nine!
At my life-stone ten times six,
Just one lustrum nearer Styx,
Wise ones say, I've lived in vain
Through life's calm and hurricane,
All my voyage wayward sport,
With no cargo brought to port,
Save upon the barren deck
Some one rescued from a wreck.
They forget that those who hold
Cargoes, houses, bonds and gold,

IMPROMPTU.

Prize pursuit and gain above
All that kindlier natures love,
And must in proportion grieve
Treasures of such cost to leave;
Churls expire without a sigh,
While 't is hard for kings to die.
But to those who "think my way,"
Death but ends a toilsome day.
Yet who may the story tell
Must avow my craft sailed well,
Though a battered hulk of wood,
Now but to dismantle good.
But a teak-built clipper thou!
Waves, for years, shall kiss thy prow,
And the winds their fury ply
Vainly on thy banner high.
Like Van Tromp's wild broom made fast,
It shall float while points the mast;
Woman's Rights and Woman's Wrongs
Still shall thrill thy fiery songs,
As of yore, in struggles grim
Brave hearts throbbed thy "Battle Hymn."

LINES WRITTEN IN A COPY OF OMAR KHAYYÁM.

At night among the churchyard thistles
The boy with feigned bravado whistles;
And minor chords when Omar sings
Betray his path's environings,
And show, however brave their tread
Our footsteps lead but to the dead.

As flow'ry meads delight the eye
Though, 'neath their grasses, serpents lie,
His jubilees, with rapture fair,
Conceal a dreg-note of despair.
The cold stars glisten in his rhymes,
To mock their muffled funeral chimes.

TO MY NIECE DAISY INTER-
PRETING LISZT.

HER tapering fingers from the keys
Purloined such dulcet harmonies,
That scarce the drowsy chords awoke,
But seemed to murmur in their sleep,
Until like troops when day hath broke,
To arms at the reveille who leap,
Her touch aroused an unseen host,
The voices of a Pentecost,
A host that in consent obeyed
The incantation of the maid.

But how portray the spirit's mood
Controlling that melodious brood?
Hath Fancy moulded yet a shape
Worthy her tenderness to drape,

TO MY NIECE DAISY.

As in those years of dolls and toys
The mimicry of later joys?
Or is she the unconscious bird
Which sings, and cares not to be heard?

Ah, no, the eager chords relate
The feelings glad or desolate
Of one whose wayward life hath been
A mystery to his fellow-men;
A monarch in the realms of tone,
Now cinctured by a priestly zone,
Who every gamut, every scale,
To Alpine height from Alpine dale,
In human life hath sobbed or sung.

As brooks in pensive beauty glide
To mingle in the breakers' roar,
But homeward with the turning tide
Some truant drops regain the shore,—
So he, his native hills among,
Now tunes the lyre his life hath strung.
And that wild life to her unknown
Her fingers trace; as on the stone

That marks a grave its legend sad
We read, nor know the good or bad
That throbbed and wrought ere tearless Death
Laid low the crumbling frame beneath.

TO EDGAR ALLAN POE.

O WAYWARD, weird, and mystic soul,
    Whose meteoric pace
Outstripped the pigmy orbs that roll
    In grooves of commonplace;
Like aerolites from heaven that fall
    Thy works were tossed and piled,
Thy Raven brooding over all,—
    Fit crest for sorrow's child.

Hadst thou been born when heroes reigned,
    And hailed the bard a seer,
A poet's largesse thou hadst gained,
    And stepped a prince's peer;
Or e'en to-day when keener thirst
    For deeper fountains longs,
Beneath thy magic touch had burst
    A Horeb of high songs.

But on thee lay the curse of toil,
    The child-devouring sire,
For life's imperious needs to moil,
    And drop the golden lyre.
Yet its rare raptures round us float,
    As of a cindered star,
Dead aeons since, the rays remote
    Still reach us from afar.

TO WALT WHITMAN.

HE who scorns the tuneful measure
  Is a lout,
Trampling down melodious pleasure
  With a shout,
Like the Moenads Corybantic,
  Who would tear
Beauty's eyelids in their frantic,
  Wild despair.
Let the Muses nine deny him,
  As a churl
Only hut-ward fit to hie him,
  From the whirl
Of the striving cadence leading
  Up the dance,
Lads and lasses gaily speeding
  In its trance.

Cornu Mirum's brassy snorting
>   Calls the kine,
But Apollo's lyre exhorting
>   The divine
Wavy swaying to its playing
>   Is a bliss,
Kindling summer-lightnings straying
>   Till they kiss.
Walt in Belvedere Apollo
>   Sees a boy
Only fit the chase to follow
>   With youth's joy.
Fool! yon tankard's crystal shimmer
>   Hides a wine
Fit for Juno, or the dimmer
>   Proserpine.
And the Bow-god, lithe and slender,
>   Hath a soul,
Mortal feelings fierce or tender
>   To control.
Sparks your darling Vulcan dashes
>   At each blow,
Only gleam to sink in ashes
>   Down below,

While the Day-god's silver lyre
    Trills its pæan
To the ultramundane choir
    Empyrean,
Voicing homage to the warder,
    Who on high
Out of chaos marshals order
    In the sky.

IMPROMPTU IN AN ALBUM.

O PEN ! wert thou a magic brush,
    And mine a limner's hand,
Upon this page what scenes should gush,—
    What skies from fairy-land !

But such bright visions fade away
    As clouds in ocean sink,
When I to thee can only pay
    My compliments in ink.

SIRO DELMONICO.

He lieth low whose constant art
For years the daily feasts purveyed
Of wayfarers from every mart,
The Paladins of every trade.

And yet to-night gay music stirs
The halls he strolled through yestere'en,
And mantles high the wine that spurs
The revellers by him unseen.

Le Roi est mort! Vive le Roi!
One leader drops, another comes;
On flows the dance,—a stream of joy
Staccatoed by the muffled drums

That soon for us shall mark the tread
Of mourning friends and chanting priests.
Ah ! there are other banquets spread
Than Siro's memorable feasts.

III.

K

FRUITION.

[JUNE.]

LIE thou there, black pack of care,
   I have carried full months nine !
Let me seek the greenwood fair
   While the summer's glory's mine.

Far from me the miser's lot—
   Beadle of a golden shrine—
Whilst, by nature's toil begot,
   All the summer's wealth is mine.

In the masquerade of flowers
   Let the Cedar, Larch, and Pine,
Mourn stern winter's vanished towers,
   So the summer's joy be mine.

FRUITION.

Ninety times the sun shall rise
    Earlier from his couch of brine,
And shall linger in the skies
    While the summer's bliss is mine.

By the stream, as when a child,
    Shrinking from the snake-like vine,
I will wander, thrush-beguiled,
    While the summer's glory's mine.

Sunbeams jewelling the showers
    Which the knotted clouds untwine
Over thirsty fields and bowers,
    Are the summer's gems and mine.

Strolling through its paths of bliss
    Skirted by the jessamine,
I will sing and dance and kiss
    While the summer's glory's mine;

Till the grapes the robins spare
    Shall redeem their pledge in wine,
Let me glean the treasures rare
    Of the summer's sparkling mine.

LEAVES AND STARS.

[SEPTEMBER.]

YESTERDAY, when Autumn's fire
Flushed the maple and the briar,
Till they crimsoned as a maid
Who her love hath just betrayed,—
Disappeared my summer dream,
Like the picture in a stream
Which the wanton breezes chase
From the liquid mirror's face.

Was each reddening leaf the ghost
Of a precious moment lost?
Else why should the woodland's glow
Thrill me with such sense of woe,

That from Summer's dying bed,
Like a frightened boy I fled,
Hastening to the changeless town
With its stony smile and frown?

Vain the coward hope! For night
Brought a monitor in sight
Sterner than those dying leaves,
Sadder than September's sheaves.
Lo! Orion stalks between
Aldebaran and the sheen
Sparkling Sirius, in disdain,
Sheds upon the Warrior's train.

Warrior—Hunter! Like a bird
Serpent-charmed, thy blazing sword
Holds me as it were the blade
O'er a prisoned monarch swayed.
Sword of menace! Blade of fear,
Shearing from my life a year!
Shall I see thee gleam again
O'er another twelvemonth slain?

OCTOBER LAY.

I.—NATURE.

STORMY day of mid October !
Nature sees thy blasts disrobe her
    Forests of their charms ;
Sees, like sparks from forges flying,
Fall the leaves of Summer dying
    In gray Autumn's arms.

As a mother to her tender
Babes her raiment doth surrender
    In the wintry hours ;
Busy in the tempest's watches,
With a quilt of many patches,
    Covers she the flowers.

As escape the wingéd legions
Of the air, from Arctic regions,
    Pale with sunless cold ;
Gales in search of tropic fires
Rushing, wake the thousand lyres
    Of the Druid wold.

Green, midst Autumn's fading splendour,
Swing the lonely willow's tender
    Fringes, o'er the brook ;
As though, fresh from Ocean's portal,
Some fair Nereid immortal
    There her ringlets shook.

Circling zephyrs, with caresses,
Gently sway those drooping tresses
    Sheltered by the grove ;
Whilst its giant tree-tops, braving
Ruder blasts, are madly waving
    In the air above.

II.—MAN.

STORMY day of mid October !
I, poor drunkard, waxing sober,
    Feel thy pelting rain
Fierce as shot my cheeks assailing,
Driven by the blast whose wailing
    Heralds Winter's reign.

As I plod with weary measure,
Conscience tolls the knell of pleasure;
    Oh, the Summer hours !
Gone are now their joys enchanting,
Leaving only phantoms, haunting
    Memory's leafless bowers.

On the leaves the wayside strewing,
I, in each a moment rueing,
    Look with tearful eyes ;
Look, as were they corpses serried
On a battle-field, ere buried
    Never more to rise.

Blows the north-wind sharp and biting,
Scatters dreams of bliss inviting,
    Rain-drops burn like fire,
And the fire my breast tormenting,
Unextinguished, unrelenting,
    Withers all desire.

Though like spray from storm-lashed surges,
Whip the forest's leaves thy scourges,
    Fearful Hurricane !
Leaflets, erst Spring's welcome bringing,
To the willow fondly clinging,
    Bright as hope remain.

SONG OF THE WREN.

The summer's joyous warblers away
    Have flown from November's frown,
And midst the palsied woodland's decay,
I reign on my perch of hemlock spray,
    A monarch without a crown.

In early spring came the Oriole
    To foster her orange brood,
Ere crept the rattlesnake from his hole
Or the dormant Owl his stern patrol
    Resumed, in the tropic wood.

The Throstle brown and the Catbird gray,
    With the timid Redbreast came,
And the Blackbird and the Bobolink gay,
With answering notes took up the lay
    Of the Grosbeak's throat of flame.

SONG OF THE WREN.

Out of last year's leaves and grasses sere
 And the gray rock's mossy beard,
In tufts, or copses shrouding the mere,
Or 'neath the Catalpa's flapping ear,
 Their nests they merrily reared.

While lasted the spring-tide's quickening hours
 Their carols the forest thrilled,
They summoned the bee to opening flowers
When honey, from April's balmy showers,
 The sun in their cups distilled.

To quiet their nestlings' plaintive cry
 Like flashes they clave the air,
Now chasing the golden dragon-fly,
Now preying upon the insect fry,
 Or the spider in his lair.

Like guests who flit from a summer fête,
 Aweary of dance and play,
Ere the motley fireworks scintillate,
In starry pennons, before the gate
 Of night, and awake the day;

SONG OF THE WREN.

They fled when the hoarfrost first congealed
    On the clover's flower-reft blade,
And Autumn her tawny dyes revealed
In the scattered spoils by road and field
    Of the Summer's masquerade.

They fled as worldly parasites fly
    From the prodigal's dying bed,
And the only mourner left am I
To witness the funeral pageantry
    Of Nature burying her dead.

The squirrel sleeps in the hollow tree
    Or munches his winter store,
The partridge crops fat berries in glee,
The quail roams gleaning the stubble free,
    And the meadow-lark the moor.

When spread the Oak his pall o'er the flowers,
    The silver Maple grew pale,
And a crimson flushed the ivied bowers
Where 'neath the Dogwood, in fervid hours
    Had blossomed the Orchis frail.

SONG OF THE WREN.

The Hickory's green to gold then turned,
    Yet clave to the fruitful bough,
While the Catbriar, as a miser spurned
In death, was stripped of its leaves, which burned
    Like coals in the muddy slough.

The Gum's leaves will with the rainbow vie,
    Till from the Heavens, o'ercast
With frowns no longer checked by the eye
Of the sun, rebellious snows shall fly
    On the ruthless Arctic blast.

But his realms their absent Lord again,
    In Spring, shall awake from sleep,
And my sisters will cheer their little Wren
With newest songs from the grove and glen,
    Where the mocking-birds vigil keep.

ORCHARD FANTASIA.

BEHOLD yon hale old apple-tree,
  In its wrinkled skin with mosses bound,
Yield to the south wind's sportive glee
The blossoms it scatters recklessly,
  Like snowflakes over the ground.

Like snow in a night they will disappear,
  Absorbed by the yearning earth;
But the fruits it hath borne for many a year,
The joy of urchins far and near,
  That tree shall again bring forth.

And as those blossoms sown by the wind
  Leave germing fruits on the bounteous tree,
So gentle words and charities kind,
Though man prove thankless, leave behind
  Sweet germs for the hoards of memory.

And when deathward sighs the bosom heaves,
  Though the kindly deeds we have done on earth
Should seem to us but as withered leaves,
While our sins, like serpents, in living sheaves,
  Daunt the soul on the verge of its second birth;

The blossoms shall flower in Heaven again,
  Where no wild breeze shall waft them away;
And the clang of the blow that breaks our chain
Shall drive the emblems of sin and pain,
  The serpents, back to their dens of clay.

IV.

L

A WAKING DREAM.

WESTWARD gazing through my window, Venus shone ;
Lit the room where I had all night dreamed alone ;
Woke her lustrous eye the slumbering depths of mine,
Kindling sparks among the ashes of lang-syne.
Vainly strove the dawn's first glories through the gloom ;
Like my heart, the lonely chamber looked a tomb
Where sweet ghosts, in sad procession, seemed to flow
Past my bed, become a bier, and there bestow

Grief's last kiss upon my brow.—Each tender glance
Thrilled my soul with joy and pain; as in a trance
Shrank within my palsied lips all utterance.
Fading in the dawn the Morn-Star disappears,
And dispels the tender throng, but not my tears;
For I wake with sorrowing heart and aching head,—
Wake to find sweet Venus vanished and Love dead.

THE INCOMPLETE PICTURE.

LAST summer, in the Catskill range,
   I took a sketch, and thought it good,
Of yonder dale,—and now 't is strange,
   The picture chimes not with my mood.

And yet the brush's motley trace
   Repeats the landscape to my eye;
The hills, with grave or smiling grace
   Of chiselled profile, fret the sky.

The knoll still shrinks beyond the lawn
   To nothingness 'twixt loftier steeps,
Gay creepers on the cottage fawn,
   And o'er the brook the willow weeps.

THE INCOMPLETE PICTURE.

The unchained skiff upon the bank
   Its shoulder rests, as in a doze;
The oars press down the rushes dank,
   The lake with yellow sunset glows.

Yon urchin toward the water sways
   His oxen, lightened of their yoke;
The air they breathe is autumn's haze,
   Or Indian summer's chilly smoke.

Yet,—like some tune that wakes no more,
   Though sweetly sung in after years,
Emotions which it roused of yore,
   The dance's throb, the burial's tears,—

My canvas mirror, tame and cold,
   Lacks sleeping Nature's living glow;
Like shrouds its shadows wrap the wold,
   Nor with the sunset seem to grow.

Ah! now I see its chief defect;
   My hand refused, beneath the porch,
To seat the lass with garlands decked
   Whose eyes took up day's fading torch.

THE TRYST.

An hour too early in the grove!
    An hour for blissful dreams,
Which countless starry eyes above
    Will gladden with their beams.

Through leaves and twigs they peep at me,
    Like frolic elves at play,
Who slip behind rock, bush, or tree,
    Whene'er one looks their way.

The varying screen through which I gaze,
    Fantastic shapes assumes,
As with its breath the south wind sways
    The tree-tops' yielding plumes;

Till rests my wandering glance upon
    The steadfast star of Jove,
As lovers' eyes all others shun
    Save those that drink their love.

I hearken to the village chime ;
    The first half-hour is past !
With what a funeral march old Time
    Sets forth upon the last !

A dark cloud sailing by puts out
    My lone star's radiant light ;
Its shadow dims with sombre doubt
    Fond hopes just now so bright.

Anon, upon the thirsty leaves
    The pattering rain-drops fall,
The sky its swelling bosom heaves
    And clouds each other call.

In place of heaven's fair face, alive
    With kindly twinkling eyes,
Remote volcanoes seem to rive
    The cloud-peaks of the skies,

THE TRYST.

Up-flaring, like the beacon's flame,
    Which darts from crag to brow
On Alpine summits, and the gleam
    Of arms reveals below.

The zephyr that with fond caress,
    The prostrate leaves just stirred,
Until methought her rustling dress
    And fairy foot I heard,—

Like a startled hind, now holds its breath,
    As the north wind's eager pant
With a hiss, as of serpents bristling its path,
    Comes driving the rain aslant;

Swaying the saplings of the wood
    And its giants of stalwart form,
Who toss their arms, like a multitude
    Applauding the voice of the storm.

Soon from the battlements of night,
    Fierce lightning shafts are hurled,
Like meteors pre-Adamite
    In the old chaotic world.

THE TRYST.

A roar, as of a smitten shield,
   Responds to those red brands,
As when Salmoneus scorned to yield
   To Jove's divine commands.

A roar as of caissons over a vault—
   Each armed with a loaded gun—
Which on its summit a moment halt,
   Then topple down one by one.

They are fired, first singly, and then pell-mell,
   And the startled air is riven
By thunder crashes like echoes from Hell
   Of its fiends besieging Heaven!

Appalled, I clasp in pallid dismay
   The tryst-tree in the glade,
While gods and Titans in frantic affray
   Ply round me their cannonade.

When lo! in the midst of that riot fell,
   Through its bolts of deadly fire,
The silvery voice of the midnight bell
   Speaks from the village spire.

THE TRYST.

As waived by a spell, the battle turns ;
  Its wild alarums cease ;
The full moon now in the zenith burns ;
  All nature is at peace.

At chime the twelfth, my whispered name,—
  And then—an angel's kiss !
Who would not brave that fearful dream
  For the wealth of this waking bliss ?

TO CONSUELO.

A SUBTILE charm bewildered me,
    As in a depth of wood
No scent of moss, or flower, or tree,
But the soft air that blends the three
    Inspires a dreamy mood.

Eyes pensive 'neath their fringe's shade,
    Sedate lips which disclosed
The pearly keys on which were played
Clear words that in me music made
    And gentlest thoughts disposed.

A vestal shape framed to entrance
    Sculptors from Phidias down,
Allure an Exarch to the dance,
Or fire the bravest knightly lance
    That e'er won tourney's crown.

TO CONSUELO.

But how shall tongue or pencil tell,
    Or eye the secret learn,
Of that unseen electric spell
Which made the heart renascent swell,
    The soul with transport burn?

Yet were I mad to analyse
    The mainsprings of a joy;
Yon magic gewgaw children prize
Draws tears if we anatomise
    And disenchant the toy.

Sweet mystery! this photograph,
    In twilight caught, is thine;
Beneath I write its epigraph,
"The precious cup I may not quaff,
    But I can bless the wine!"

NOT WINE ALONE.

'TIS not within the vine-wreathed bowl
   Alone, that madness lies.
Whatever quickens pulse and soul,
Beyond sage reason's mild control,
   With wine's sweet frenzy vies.

The Boy, when first his arrow shakes
   Within the circle's eye ;
The Youth, whose javelin o'ertakes
The roebuck bounding to the brakes,
   Is drunk with ecstasy.

The Rider, when his steed hath past
   Some rival cavalcade ;
And he whose bark and wind-bent mast
On adverse sails their shadows cast,
   In sport or cannonade ;

The brain that yields to starry eyes,
  Or fires with clash of steel;
Or swims when victory's shouts arise
From blood-stained fields to evening skies,—
  All these with madness reel.

The Bard, whose fervid strains arouse
  Ten thousand echoes, when
A nation's gratitude endows
With laurel or with oak the brows
  Of King or Citizen;

The Conqueror, with sheathéd sword,
  'Midst Io Pæans borne;
The Tribune, whose electric word,
Upon the forum's billows poured,
  Awakens wrath or scorn;—

These all are drunk with conscious power,
  And they, the fierce or cold,
Who revel in revenge's hour,
Or who exult when gloating o'er
  Red piles of hidden gold.

Yet, when I glow with gladdening wine,
All, all these various joys are mine
    At Fancy's will.
Love, beauty, fame, rank, wealth, and power,
Alternate, in the jocund hour
    My bosom fill.

Again, a boy, I clutch the prize,
A youth, I bask in sunny eyes,
    The race I win;
My bark all other barks outstrips,
My name is, by a nation's lips,
    Made Glory's twin.

'Tis o'er! I find 'twas but a dream.
But through the fore-dawn's dark extreme,
    Day's earliest dart
Reminds me that, in Love or War,
Such triumphs leave no other scar
    Than in my heart.

THE RUBY GOBLET.

Comrades ! we have sung and laughed
　Merrily to-night ;
Each of us a cup hath quaffed
　To his mistress bright.
Do not let a sadder strain
　Take you by surprise ;
Ere the toast we fill again
　I would moralise.

Blazoned in our firmament
　Float the poiséd hours,
From their task, like us, unbent,
　Garlanded with flowers.
In this polished table's face
　See the wax-lights gleam,
As the early sunbeams chase
　Darkness from a stream.

THE RUBY GOBLET.

Say, is not this empty glass
    Some poor spirit's jail?
Else, when I my finger pass
    Round it, why this wail?
Now a maiden's plaintive sigh,
    Now a captive's groan,
Now a stricken warrior's cry
    Seems its swelling tone.

These dim arabesques you see
    Gild its ruddy bowl,
Are the faded tracery
    Of a magic scroll.
Mine the wizard's mystic lore
    To divine the spell,
And evoke those shapes of yore
    From the crystal cell.

Hist! an echo now replies
    Faintly to my hymn;
Lo! a ghost with pale blue eyes
    Rises to the brim.

Wistful is his visage cold,
   Trimmed his beard with grace,
As we see in many an old
   Pictured knightly face.

To my ear those lips so pale,
   In his native tongue
Whisper now a sadder tale
   Than our lips have sung.
'Tis a century at least
   Since Venetian mould
Fashioned for his bridal feast
   This red cup I hold.

Day had only broken thrice
   Ere the Adriatic,
Of his young heart's Paradise
   Quenched the bliss ecstatic.
Ransomed came from Tunis' strand
   One long mourned as dead,
By whose madly jealous hand
   His fair life was sped.

Though she wept and tore her hair
   On her darling's bier,
Fugitive was her despair
   As the fleeting year.
Hardly was the crimson dried
   On the fatal knife,
Ere became the victim's bride
   The destroyer's wife.

From this chalice, which her lips
   Drained their bridal night,
He, in spirit hovering, sips
   Still a sad delight.
Hark! the spectre chants a lay
   Of the olden time—
Listen, while my lips essay
   To repeat the rhyme.

All the friends who round my bridal board
   Joyous shone,
Are, like me, beneath the tufted sward,
   Dead and gone.

THE RUBY GOBLET.

Oft has this beloved goblet rung
 Life's first dawn;
Often wailed the child whose birth it sung,
 Dead and gone.

Warriors I have seen, and statesmen hoary,
 Round it drawn;
Seen eclipsed their wisdom and their glory,
 Dead and gone.

Jovial guests! how near your notes of glee,
 Those lips yawn,
To swallow you as they have swallowed me,
 Dead and gone.

  Comrades! sadly sings the ghost
    Of this ruby glass;
  Fill to him a silent toast—
    Quick the flagon pass.
  If so near the red lips yawn
    Of the glutton grave,
  Let us antedate the dawn
    In this rosy wave!

BOHEMIAN SONG.

Come, trip it with me gaily here,
   The forest glade our ball-room is,
The ills of life shall disappear,
   Or from the turf rebound in bliss.

Blow, comrade, blow thy wheaten pipe,
   Twang, brother, twang the trembling string,
Care gripes us with an iron gripe;—
   To care the joyous heel we fling.

Their walls of stone but dungeons are,
   To those who in great cities dwell,
'Neath roofs through which no sunbeam fair
   Can reach the flowers we love so well.

For us our last night's grassy bed
   Kind nature makes up fresh again,
Ere drops the sun his weary head
   Upon the bosom of the main.

In sleep we hear the mystic powers
   Of earth their subtile callings ply;
Awake, in brighter worlds than ours,
   We read the marvels of the sky.

Once more, sweet partner, pipe again;
   Twang fiercer, mates, the cittern's call;
For unseen spirits swell the strain
   To which our feet keep festival.

An atom less, and we should be
   Floating on rosy clouds of love;
A feather more, with pinions free,
   Cleaving the paths of worlds above.

Thy drooping head my shoulder seeks,
   Sweet partner of the wandering doom
Which poised 'twixt earth and heaven keeps
   Us like Mohammed's pensile tomb.

BOHEMIAN SONG.

The evening star sinks fast, and see !
    Around us in the twilight shades,
The mystic throngs of old Chaldee,
    Her patriarchs, matrons, braves and maids.

Blow softly while the ghostly crew
    The cadence mark with statelier pace ;
Are they so many—we so few ?
    O brothers, quick, one warm embrace !

They're gone ! 'tis night ; at dusk they come,
    Those shades of our long-buried sires,
To follow us where'er we roam ;
    Now, comrades ! to your evening fires.

WALTZ.

COME to me, maiden fair,
Maiden with golden hair,
Now that the vesper air
Trembles no more with prayer!

Come where the Zingaree,
Under the linden tree,
Spurring his comrades three,
Pipes a wild jubilee!

Come, while their tabor's beat
Urges the dancers fleet;
Come, let thy tiny feet
Mine on the meadow meet!

Bounding we gaily start;
Flashes thy blue eyes dart:
Spare thou my captive heart;
Or—let us never part!

Strains gently sighing in the air, love,
Wake echoes in our hearts so near, love!
    I pant with thy sighs,
    And see with thine eyes.
Swayed by the magic waltz, love,
Ne'er to its measure false, love,
    One hand in thine,
    One holds thee mine,
Mine, while fills the glade the whirling dance,
    With visions bright
    That dazzle sight;
Mine, while clasped we float, as in a trance,
    On pinions bright
    This sparkling night.

Rarest diamonds of the mine, love,
Pale beside those eyes of thine, love;
But ere I thy hand resign,
Take, oh, take this heart of mine.

Dying, sleeps in death the strain;
Sinks my soul in gloom and pain.
Till that waltz shall wake again,
Thou and I, sweet girl, are twain.

MAZURKA.

Stand aside while Schamiloff,
In the hall of Peterhof,
Drags the Queen of Beauty off,
Duchess Olga Romanoff,
Stemming the dance's tide
With the Mazurka stride
    Which she, so lately
    Grand Duchess stately,
    Follows sedately.
Now, with a victor's pride,
    Clasps he her slender waist,
Twin-like they onward glide,
    As though by foemen chased;
Now casts her loose, but holds,
    Vice-like, her captive hand;
While like a tempest rolls
    Louder the frantic band.

He tramps with fiercer swing,
She his pace following
Lightly as bird on wing,
Follows without demur
His clashing heel and spur;
He proud as Lucifer,
She as an angel calm
Trusting his iron arm
Through the wild dances swarm,
Till the orchestral storm
Melts into melodies
Soft as a summer breeze.
Now other steps they choose,
He in his turn pursues
And her forgiveness woos,
With a beseeching joy,
Woos her retreating coy,
When, like a thunder-clap,
Halt! bids the leader's rap,
And Duchess Olga sees
Schamiloff on his knees.

DAWN AT MIDNIGHT.

ALONE upon the Spouting Rock
   I hear its voices roar,
And watch the baffled surges' shock
   Against the iron shore.

The wind grows bolder—not a cloud
   Restrains the sweeping breath
I've seen rend ships, till mast and shroud
   Whirled in a dance of death.

Against the sky, with swollen sail,
   A bark now ploughs the deep;
Her freight, perchance, but seed this gale
   Shall sow, and Ocean reap.

DAWN AT MIDNIGHT.

God speed those whom the winds pursue
   This wild yet starry night;
And keep my heart until I view
   Her casement's promised light.

Sail on, O bark, through every change
   Of season and of sky;
Within the haven of yon grange
   My hopes at anchor lie!

THE MOON AND THE BEACON.

Honey moon! Honey moon!
  Though this April night
Ocean, bay, and dark lagoon
  Revel in thy light,
Will to-morrow see thy rays
  Where to-night they gleam,
And my young bride's tender gaze
  Still with gladness beam?

Beacon light! Beacon light!
  On yon lonely shore,
Shining faith-like every night,
  Where the breakers roar,
Like a beating heart thy flash,
  Fed by human care,
Cheers the mariner when crash
  Tempests through the air.

Maiden fair! Maiden fair!
  While the orange wreath
Sheds its fragrance o'er thy hair,
  Let thy balmier breath
Vow that, like the Beacon's light,
  Thou wilt ever shine
For the lover who to-night
  Links his fate with thine.

LA CHOCOLATIÈRE.

BRIGHT are thine eyes, my pretty little maid,
　　As diamonds sunk in jet;
Brown is thy cheek, as shadows in the glade
　　By eve for lovers set.

Lissom and smooth thy fairy-moulded shape
　　Which gossamer muslins press,
As clouds around the Jungfrau's summit drape
　　Her snows with mute caress.

Sometimes a thrill shoots through the sweet repose
　　In which thou art enchained,
And like the flush of summer-lightning glows
　　Thy cheek with azure veined.

Say! dost thou then a song of spirits hear,
  Inaudible to me?
Or, on his throne in dreamland's moonlit sphere,
  Thy young heart's monarch see?

Say! if the black braids of the silken hair
  In which thy face is noosed,
Are but a witchingly-devisèd snare
  To pinion souls seduced?

For—that thy fawn eyes bait no ambuscade
  Could I but fondly trust—
I'd kneel so low to thee, O pretty maid,
  My brow should kiss the dust!

TO MY NIECE LOUISE.

DOLORES.

Her ear to all the litanies
   Of brooks and whispering leaves alive,
Pure as the violet-laden breeze,
   Dolores hath no sin to shrive.

By fawns she's welcomed in the fields;
   In groves by birds with vying throats,
To swains or lords no heed she yields,
   But in sweet peace serenely floats;

Till in the twilight hour she hears
   A voice that wakes her sleeping heart,
Now breathing tones that melt to tears,
   Now blasts at which her pulses start.

Sphinx-like her face, while tender fires
   Soften the glaciers of her breast,
And pleasing fears and new desires
   Like fairy voices thrill her rest.

Her ear thenceforth his trumpet is ;
   Her soul a lyre within his hands ;
Her eye sees only light in his
   Who twines her fate with silken strands.

TITIAN TO STELLA.

I LOVE thee that thou dost inspire
My ice-bound heart with quickening fire,
    And makest me forget,
One silver moment, that I'm old,
When warms thy breath my lips, from cold
    Indifference to regret.

As in gray autumn's dreary days
Their pallid cheeks the asters raise,
    To catch the sun's stray kiss,
So, ere the Arctic night sets in,
Thy radiance shall my last thread spin
    With rapture's golden bliss.

O thrilling touch, O glowing eyes,
Whose beams, like stars in wintry skies,

>Shine harmless on the snow!
Harmless as when, in tempest dark,
The palmer from the steel's cold spark
>>A kindling flame would blow.

>Yet—phantom dear of buried days
That veilest, with a sunset haze,
>>The future's gloom and sorrow—
Stay! that the thought of thee may bless,
With one bright ray of happiness,
>>The dark clouds of to-morrow!

"NO CARDS."

Let me wed thee where my wooing
  Sanctified this mossy glade,
Where above us ring-doves cooing
  Long their leafy nest delayed.

Do not think my soul would falter
  To proclaim thy heart my prize,
But a crowd before an altar
  Minds me of a sacrifice,

Where no Dian moved to pity
  Swift bears off the doomèd maid,
As when in the Aulic city
  Calchas dropped his baffled blade.

"NO CARDS."

Let the hermit, e'en now telling
  Soft his beads in yonder hut,
Breathe the prayer thy fears dispelling,
  Tie the knot man shall not cut.

Let no vain misgivings daunt thee,
  Freely, bravely, plight thy troth;
Wilt not have, should worldlings taunt thee,
  My sword, and yon friar's oath?

A DEPARTING BRIDE.

Steamship "Russia," *July* 6, 1873.

Her winsome face and artless grace
   Like sunbeams warmed my heart,
As angels bright diffuse a light
   That stays when they depart.

A touch may heal; a spark from steel
   Of bright eyes kindle fire;
One touch of hers my finger stirs
   To wake with joy the lyre.

And through the day her spirit gay
   Spread like a summer breeze,
When left alone, I saw her on
   The alienating seas.

A DEPARTING BRIDE.

To her my thanks. Back to the ranks,
    I turn, of work and strife,
Breathing a prayer that saints as fair
    As she, may guard her life.

LIEBESRUHE.

Slaked is the burning desert-thirst,
   And thou art wholly mine;
Stilled is the heart I thought must burst
   When throbbing close to thine.

Calmed the strange sense of vague unrest
   That shipwrecked mariners feel,
Ere, through the tropic breaker's crest,
   They launch their untried keel,

Framed of the lordly tree which gave
   Them shelter from the blast,
When, beachward high, the strong-armed wave
   Their senseless bodies cast.

Like them, my heart, life's bleakest heath
　In darkness doomed to rove,
Found rest and woke to bliss beneath
　The mantle of thy love.

With fire they carved the giant bole
　Unconscious of its fate ;
With flame I shaped thy stately soul
　To carry mine as freight.

In it, through passion's surges driven,
　I float beyond their roar ;
And we, O Love ! are nearer Heaven
　Than when we left the shore.

THE MARINER'S BETROTHED.

MORNING-STAR of drear November,
　Peering o'er yon wild lagoon,
Last thy radiance I remember,
　Sparkling on that eve in June,

As we two came forth together,
　From the porch with roses pied,
Blushed I, when he asked me whether
　I would be a sailor's bride.

Then, invoking thy soft splendour
　Lingering in the pale blue West,
Words he whispered, true and tender,
　Till I sank upon his breast.

With the twilight, ah, he vanished,
　Vanished to return in May.
Oh, 'tis sad to love one banished
　To the ocean's desert way!

But though day thy lustre hideth,
　Star of love! from morn to night
In the deep lagoon abideth
　Still thine image, truthful, bright.

And though far his bark be riding
　Friendly sea or stormy wave,
In my heart's deep springs abiding
　Shines his image fair and brave.

CATECHISM.

LOVER.

MAIDEN, whom I fain would woo,
Tell me truly—what canst do?
Nay—a moment let the lute
That just won my ear be mute,
Nor inflame my soul again
With thy voice's siren strain.
Speak me calmly—speak me true;
Candour thou shalt never rue.

MAIDEN.

I can reckon and can read,
Deftly say my prayers and creed,
In the church know when to kneel,
And will neither lie nor steal;

Thus far have been reared in ease,
Learning chiefly how to please,
And with song and merry smile,
Hours of sadness to beguile.

LOVER.

This is well, but not enough.
Life is made of sterner stuff;
From the altar dateth bliss,
From it too oft wretchedness.
Ask thy heart if it feel sure
Thou canst care and want endure—
Sorrow also—nor repine
At the lot that made them thine.

MAIDEN.

If my will and power I knew,
Me thou wouldst not seek to woo;
Were my virgin soul not wax,
Which life's stern impression lacks,
Waiting till Love's mystic seal
Stamp its fate for woe or weal,
Thou wouldst find the vow a curse,—
"Take for better or for worse."

LOVER.

Sweeter honey yield thy lips
Than the bee from clover sips,
Sweeter tones than thrill thy lute
Breathes thine answer to my suit;
Canst thou not divine my fate,
Whether bright or desolate?
Speak! for if deceived in thee,
Life and Love must bankrupt be.

MAIDEN.

Ere a charger thou dost buy,
Thou canst all his paces try;
Buy him—and if good he'll grow
With the grace thy hands bestow.
Yet the jockey's cunning task
May his imperfections mask;
If his value thou wouldst know,
Must upon a journey go.

METATHALAMIUM.

WHEN like a perfume from thy lips
   The May-Queen's Song first through me stole,
Like dawn above the mountain tips,
   Thy voice made morning in my soul,
Until expired the tender strain
   And silence quenched the rosy light,
When though I woke to day again,
   Within my spirit all was night.

When horn and viol banished thought,
   Yet summoned every sense that slept,
My hand thy grasp with ardour sought,
   And through the dance's maze we swept;
But while thy feet, with tireless tread,
   Fulfilled its orb like Dian chaste,
My reeling brain with frenzy sped,
   Until my clasp released thy waist.

We married—nor would I have changed
  My lot that morn for crown of gold.
A month has flown—are you estranged?
  I find you silent, thoughtful, cold.
I am but mortal—whilst you sang
  In blissful dreams I sat entranced,
And when the waltz its summons rang,
  Whilst I had breath and sight I danced.

But when or song or dance expires,
  A gold cord snaps—a spell is broke.
'Tis sad but true that mortal fires,
  Like those of brushwood, end in smoke.
You promised me to make life bright
  With smiles—then why that pouting glance?
You cannot sing from morn till night,
  Nor I from night till morning dance.

ZAMPITA.

Oh, she was wondrous fair,
    And when I said
    "Thee would I wed,"
She listened to my prayer;

But not as woman hears,
    When thrills the oath
    Of plighted troth
In her expectant ears;

Rather as Mary Saint
    In altared shrine,
    With look benign,
Receives a sinner's plaint

Who asks a happier lot ;
    Though to his suit
    The Virgin, mute
But gracious, answers not,

Until his soul shall rise,
    Through saving grace,
    Her living face
To meet in Paradise.

  .   .   .   .   .

I said, "When we are wed,
    My paradise
    Shall be thine eyes."
Then she—"My heart is dead."

I answered—"Only seared,
    And by the blight
    Of broken plight
To me far more endeared.

"Black is the carboneer,
    Who burns the oak
    To blacker coke,
And makes the woodlands drear.

"But blacker yet his soul,
    Who kindled thine
    With base design,
And left its blossoms coal.

"My love with tender art
    And patient aim
    Shall blow its flame
Upon thy cindered heart."

At this she dimly smiled,
    As in a grief
    One finds relief
By curious tales beguiled.

And when my suit I pressed,
    She, still in sorrow,
    Sighed, "Well, to-morrow;
Now, prithee, let me rest."

The morrow came and sealed
    Our fates in one;
    Fair smiled the sun;
Gaily the church-bells pealed.

    .   .   .   .

As when you chance to feel
    A limb of wood,
    It chills your blood,
As might the surgeon's steel;

I found the wounded pride
    Of Love's keen smart,
    Had left her heart
Not charred, but petrified.

For years I've vainly striven
    With ardour true
    To fire anew
That heart by sorrow riven.

For years my lips have tasted
    The mocking bliss
    Of marble kiss,
Until my frame is wasted.

And when I pray for death,
    Her lips, still fair,
    Add to my prayer,
Amen! with icy breath.

TODESFRAGE.

Did she ever, ever love me?
　Never, never shall I know,
Till I join her soul above me
　And her body down below.

When I sought to draw the fire
　Of affection from her eye,
Mine alone was the desire,
　Mine the smile or mine the sigh.

See her like a statue sleeping!
　Yet no colder is she now
Than when living—and my weeping
　Failed to melt her icy brow.

Yet that brow at times with flashes
    Of a cindered past relumed;
Like the runes that flare in ashes
    Of old letters just consumed.

Did its snow conceal a mystery,
    Shame or crime beneath its crust?
Or but cover up the history
    Of all human pride and dust?

For the last time let me kiss her,
    Shut the lid—I'll weep no more,
Since my heart will only miss her
    As a prisoner the door

Of his cell shut to at dawning
    To exclude all day the light,
And at eventide set yawning
    To admit a starless night.

GIVE ME JOY.

WHEN age its wrinkles and its snows
   Had laid on Talma's cheek and brow,
   'Tis said he made the mournful vow,
No friend shall see my eyes unclose;
   For every form he looked upon
   Revealed a ghastly skeleton.
This earth was bright when first, a toy,
   Life in my youthful hands was placed,
   But now its waters have no taste—
Bring me the wine-cup! Give me joy!

Like Talma, in the present dim
   And future dark, I see abound,
   In silvery age and youth just crowned
With beauty's wreath, but spectres grim.
   E'en Fortune's ingots lost and won
   Are watched by Care, the skeleton;
Nay, power, wealth, and pleasure cloy,
   'Tis all the same sad change of tone

From smile to tear, from laugh to groan—
Bring me the wine-cup ! Give me joy !

Though youth has fled, affections still
    With steady glow my heart may cheer :
    Come hither, wife and children dear,
Come, ere the cup again I fill,
    Come, ere each loved shape looked upon
    Shall seem to hide a skeleton.
What ! was thy smile but a decoy ?
    And ye to whom I've given breath,
    Do ye already wait my death ?
Quick ! quick ! The wine-cup ! Give me joy !

Begone, ye vipers whom I've nursed,
    And cherished with my heart's best blood ;
    Beldame, avaunt ! with all thy brood
And be ye all like me accurst !
    Thank Heaven, thy witching beauty's gone
    And leaves thee but a skeleton.
Come, friend beloved ! Thou since a boy
    My more than brother, thou'lt not fail !
    Away, thou death's-head grim and pale !—
Fill, fill the wine-cup ! Give me joy !

Thou'st changed the wine, my throat it burns,
    'Tis bitter as ingratitude !
    What ! say'st thou from the grape 'twas brewed ?
Within my lips to gall it turns !
    Bring me the glass ! O death, thou'st won !
    I see myself a skeleton !
And that weird shape was once a boy,
    To whom each scene below shone fair ?
    God ! How its eyeless sockets stare !
Is there no cup will give me joy ?

No, not the bowl ! The chalice bring,
    Exhaustless with the Paschal blood
    That purified sin's sable flood,
And still flows from Thee, thorn-crowned King !
    In whom mine eyes behold alone
    A Saviour, not a skeleton !
Oh, touch the hearts of wife and boy,
    And friend, with quivering grace divine.
    Thou wilt ! Then let me life resign,
Draining Thy last cup's heavenly joy !

IN FIFTH AVENUE.

My husband is neither young nor old,
    Though his hair is turning gray;
My temper is neither hot nor cold,
    Yet I mope the livelong day.

My house is neither spacious nor small;
    'Tis built in the usual way,
And nicely furnished from garret to hall,
    Yet I mope the livelong day.

We have children twain, a boy and a girl,
    My every wish they obey,
Tom's a rough diamond, Maud is a pearl,
    Yet I mope the livelong day.

Abroad I may either walk or drive,
    As it suits my humour's play;
We breakfast at nine and dine at five,
    And I mope the livelong day.

The bees that feed all winter on honey
    To flowers return in May;
All seasons are like, with plenty of money,
    Yet I mope the livelong day.

My husband's the bee that gathers the sweets,
    In sunshine he makes the hay,
And drudges in rain through muddy streets
    While I mope the livelong day.

When dinner is over, he like a drone
    On the sofa snoozes away,
And over the paper I mope alone
    At night—as I moped all day.

They called me lovely when I was young,
    And fond of praise and display;
'Tis a tale that's told and a song that's sung,
    For I mope the livelong day.

An old admirer unto me came,
    Resolved fresh homage to pay,
And tenderly sighing he whispered his flame
    As I moped at home one day.

He came just after the postman's bell—
    My husband was far away—
And when he swore that he loved me well,
    I moped no more that day.

An Indian god in a jewelled shrine
    Condemned for ever to stay,
Like me—if alive—would mope and pine
    When alone the livelong day.

From worship to earthly love is a stride—
    A stage without a relay—
The abrupt transition touched my pride,
    And I moped no more that day.

He seized my hand and I felt a spark,
    His eye shot a wicked ray
Which I sometimes see again in the dark,
    When I've moped the livelong day.

Though I forgave him he wanted still more;
    I scorned my vows to betray,
But ordered him to be shown the door,
    And moped no more that day.

And I sometimes wish that this stupid life
  Might finish without delay;
I'm a virtuous, uncomplaining wife,
  But I mope the livelong day.

And when to our marble church we go,
  I wonder why people pray,
For I have everything here below,
  Yet I mope the livelong day.

TO A WELL-KNOWN CAMELLIA.

PRAY, who was Lady Hume? and why her
 blush?
Was it a sad or sweet emotion
Which wakened on her cheek this earliest flush
 Of dawn awakening the ocean?

Was it the voice of homage women prize,
 Or undreamt love's abrupt confession?
Or did the mute reproach of sorrowing eyes
 Beyond all speech make intercession?

Was it the flash of anger half controlled,
 Or shame's ill-maskéd hue of panic?
Or the resentment of a virtue bold
 Withstanding passion's burst volcanic?

TO A WELL-KNOWN CAMELLIA.

We'll hope that she, whose name upon thy
  bloom
  All princes shall outlast and powers,
Lacked not a soul her beauty to perfume
  Like thee, O Queen! but of the scentless
  flowers;

That like the matron fair I may not name,
  Her blush betrayed a soul transcending
Her charms, and through them glowing to
  proclaim
  Its grace with their effulgence blending.

UNDERGRADUATE.

Gentle maiden ! whom sixteen
    Summers drape with statelier grace
Than thy mirror's placid sheen
    Held when first I saw thy face ;
Thou art now as one awaiting
    To be ferried o'er the stream,
Ever narrowing and abating,
    That divides thee from thy dream ;

Waiting till some glorious morn
    That young ferryman appears,
At the notes of whose sweet horn
    Hopes and blushes come with fears ;
Then his shallop he unmooring,
    Arrow-like shall speed to thee,
And thy foot scarce touch the flooring
    Ere he whispers, "Come with me !"

" Not across the shrinking river,
   But adown its channel mid
To the island where forever,
   Nestling as the doves lie hid,
I may tell thee how I love thee,
   While thou answerest, *Love me more*,
Till my tenderness shall prove thee
   Wisely to have left the shore."

IMPROMPTU.

TO MISS S. W. ON THE RIGI.

EDELWEISS, Edelweiss,
Edelweiss was she,
Budding on that mountain top
Far above the sea !
Edelweiss, Edelweiss,
Edelweiss again,
Scarce a new moon later
Blooming in the plain.
Edelweiss upon the Rigi
Lilienweiss upon the lea,
Fifty years have dug the chasm
That divideth her from me !

In the valley as I stood
Gray and owl-like by the wood,

IMPROMPTU.

She a lily 'gainst the green
On her stately stem was seen ;
A child's the heart within her bodice
Yet in face and form a goddess,
I could pray, yes, pray and kneel,
Die, if need were, for her weal.
Gamblers rather lose their all
Than forsake the mocking ball,
And to love is greater gain
Than not being loved is pain.

Edelweiss, Edelweiss,
On the Jungfrau steep !
Snows as pure as where I pluck thee
Shall thy starry petals keep ;
And a happier lot betide thee
Where thy sister fair shall hide thee
Than amidst the snows eternal
Of thy glacier home supernal !
For this bettering of thy fortune
Let thy gratitude importune
Her to breathe a gentle *Ave*,
For the soul of him that gave thee.

TO GRACE.

Sable her garb as starless skies,
   A harvest moon her face,
Twin glories sparkled in her eyes,
   Her lips blushed bounteous grace.
And when they moved, her voice so soft
   And musical in tone,
Seemed Dian's floating from aloft
   To wake Endymion.

Ah! would I were that sleeping boy,
   Unconscious of the bliss
Awaiting him when love its joy
   Shall pour through Dian's kiss!
Nor did it chill my longing mood
   To realise that I,
Were such a kiss by Grace bestowed,
   Should not awake—but die!

Catskill, *August* 22, 1874.

THE VALLEY-LILY.

Take, O Gardener, to the maiden
   In whose praise the harp I string,
Take at dawn a basket laden
   With the loveliest blooms of spring.
Let no orange-flowers suggesting
   Altar, priest, or ring be there,
But sweet valley-lilies, cresting
   Roses than her cheek less fair;

Seeing which, her bird with mellow
   Throat shall pipe a roundelay,
And her eyelids from her pillow
   Open on a happy day,
Happier should its waning prove her
   Mindful of the tender stress
That impels my soul to love her,
   Though that love she never bless.

SONG.

My Sibyl hath a dainty look
    Of spiritual grace,
Serene as yonder limpid brook
    That ripples through the chase;

Where, when at night the merry stars
    Upon its waters play,
Their peering eyes find naught that mars
    Its clearness through the day.

But they at dawn their glories hide,
    Whilst Sibyl's look benign
Beams fair, as 'neath that mimic tide
    Its sun-kissed pebbles shine.

V.

LE MANOIR DE LOCKSLEY.

An experiment.

Amis ! Je veux attendre ici que pâlisse l'aurore ;
Laissez-moi ! Quand vous me voudrez, donnez du cor sonore.

C'est bien toi ! Manoir de Locksley. Autour, comme jadis,
Au long des dunes l'on entend se héler les courlis.

Locksley ! tes tours dominent les coteaux jusqu'au rivage,
Et le flot-billon déferle en dentelles sur la plage.

Que de nuits m'ont vu, là, sous cette ogive contempler,
Au couchant, le grand Orion lentement s'incliner ;

Ou le lever, dans la brume qui coiffe les collines,
Des essaims de mouches à feu, par files argentines.

Dans ces landes ma jeunesse féerique s'abreuvait
Des merveilles de science que le Temps nous transmet :

Quand les siècles passés reposaient comme un champ fécond,
Faisant croire aux promesses que le présent cache au fond :

Je scrutai l'avenir, autant que l'œil humain pénètre,
Depuis le fait actuel jusqu'à la merveille à naître.

Le printemps cramoisit à neuf la gorge du robin ;
Le printemps donne une autre huppe au vanneau libertin.

Au printemps plus vif en ses couleurs le ramier s'agite ;
Au printemps le jouvenceau d'un amour soudain palpite.

De son beau visage amaigri se fanaient les appas,
Et son regard muet ne faisait qu'épier mes pas.

Ce que voyant je dis : " Ne me caches rien, chère Aimée,
Tout mon cœur tend vers toi comme au rivage la marée."

De son œil alangui jaillit un éclair éphémère,
Vermeil comme quand l'Ourse déploie au Nord sa bannière.

Puis j'observai le trouble de son sein à mes aveux,
Et son âme dans les sombres profondeurs de ses yeux.

"J'ai voilé, Cousin, mes sentiments de peur de me nuire ;
"M'aimes-tu ?" fit-elle en pleurs. "Longtemps je l'ai voulu dire."

L'amour prit le sablier du temps dans ses doigts ardents,
Et, le tournant, en sable d'or fit couler les moments ;

L'amour fit tant d'arpéges sur la harpe de la Vie,
Que le ton du Soi, tremblant, s'absorba dans l'harmonie.

Souvent, la cognée au bois, le matin nous surprenait,
Des fièvreux transports du printemps sa voix me remplissait ;

Souvent, lorsque à se croiser les voiles nous contemplâmes,
Au doux contact des lèvres se confondirent nos âmes.

O cousine ! Aimée ! O cœur léger ! mon éternel deuil !
Lande morne ! Triste rive où la vague bat l'écueil !

Fonds où ne saurait atteindre la sonde du poète !
D'un regard dur, d'un mot vif, docile marionnette !

Dois-je croire que, m'ayant connu, tu trouves le bonheur
En t'abaissant au rang plus bas d'émotions, de cœur ?

AT LAST.

WHAT care I whence the cold wind blows,
 Or if yon skies be drear,
Now that my longing arms enclose
 Her whom I hold most dear!

What care I for the wealth and power
 That light an emperor's throne,
Since that kiss made—'tis scarce an hour—
 Those tender lips my own!

Let warriors chase the phantom-light
 Of glory o'er the field,
And tyrants with oppression's might
 Make sullen nations yield.

ENFIN.

Qu'importe d'où vient la bise
    Qui teint en gris les cieux,
Puisqu'enfin, dans mes bras, Elise
    Répond à tous mes vœux !

Qu'importent la puissance et l'or
    Qui luisent près d'un roi,
Puisque, cédés leurs doux trésors,
    Ses lèvres sont à moi !

De la gloire que le soldat
    Cherche le feu follet,
Et de son sceptre les appas
    Le tyran détesté.

Let orators with stormy breath
    Upheave the human seas,
And heirs rejoice when pallid death
    Gives them the golden keys.

I'll henceforth live alone for her
    Who lives alone for me;
The vine that clasps the hoary fir
    Makes glad the lonely tree.

What though death lurk in its embrace,—
    Both men and trees must die;
What matters then my resting-place,
    Or when in it I lie?

Her tears shall bless with flowers my grave,
    Until her soul take wing;
As o'er the fallen fir shall wave
    The vine-bells many a spring.

ENFIN.

Que l'orateur, comme l'orage,
    Soulève l'assemblée,
Et l'ainé, de son héritage,
    Touche la clef dorée.

Désormais pour elle je vis
    Qui pour moi seul existe ;
La vigne verte autour de lui
    Réjouit le sapin triste.

Que ses baisers cachent la mort,—
    Tout sapin doit mourir ;
Qu'importe quand le même sort
    Me condamne à périr ?

Ses pleurs éclateront en roses
    Dessus mon toit dernier ;
Comme, du pin couchant écloses,
    Les fleurs de vigne en Mai.

LA SYLPHIDE.

Béranger.

La Raison a son ignorance ;
Son flambeau n'est pas toujours clair ;
Elle niait votre existence,
Sylphes charmants, peuples de l'air ;
Mais, écartant sa lourde égide
Qui gênait mon œil curieux,
J'ai vu naguère une sylphide,
Sylphes légers, soyez mes dieux.

Oui, vous naissez au sein des roses,
Fils de l'Aurore et des Zéphyrs ;
Vos brillantes métamorphoses
Sont le secret de nos plaisirs.

THE SYLPHIDE.

From the French of Béranger.

IGNORANT, at times, is Reason,
   And her torch not always clear ;
She denies,—fair Sylphs, what treason !—
   That your people fill the air ;
Her huge Ægis pushed aside,
   One bright glimpse beyond to steal,
Once a Sylphide I descried,
   Now to none but Sylphs I kneel.

Born and nurtured amid roses,
   Children of the morning breeze,
Your untold metempsychoses
   Charm us in all things that please ;

D'un souffle vous séchez nos larmes ;
Vous épurez l'azur des cieux :
J'en crois ma sylphide et ses charmes.
Sylphes légers, soyez mes dieux.

J'ai deviné son origine
Lorsqu'au bal, ou dans un banquet,
J'ai vu sa parure enfantine
Plaire par ce qui lui manquait.
Ruban perdu, boucle défaite,
Elle était bien, la voilà mieux.
C'est de vos sœurs la plus parfaite.
Sylphes légers, soyez mes dieux.

Que de grâce en elle font naître
Vos caprices toujours si doux !
C'est un enfant gâté peut-être,
Mais un enfant gâté par vous.
J'ai vu sous un air de paresse,
L'amour rêveur peint dans ses yeux.
Vous qui protégez la tendresse,
Sylphes légers, soyez mes dieux.

THE SYLPHIDE.

With a breath our tears you dry,
   You the rainbow's hues reveal,
Yours the azure of the sky;
   Ah! to none but Sylphs I kneel!

I my Sylphide's race divined
   When upon the ball-room's floor,
She, untrammelled as the wind,
   Won more hearts the less she wore;
Loosened bow-knot, tangled hair
   Did but beauties fresh reveal;
Fairest she among the fair
   Of the Sylphs to whom I kneel.

Ah! in her what grace engender
   All your fancies sweet and new,
Spoilt she is—I can't defend her,
   But the darling's spoilt by you.
In her languid moments even
   'Neath her lids see Cupid steal,
Open them—and earth is heaven!
   Now to none but Sylphs I kneel.

Mais son aimable enfantillage
Cache un esprit aussi brillant
Que tous les songes qu'au bel âge
Vous nous apportez en riant.
Du sein de vives étincelles
Son vol m'élevait jusqu'au cieux ;
Vous dont elle empruntait les ailes,
Sylphes légers, soyez mes dieux.

Hélas ! rapide météore,
Trop vite elle a fui loin de nous.
Doit-elle m'apparaître encore ?
Quelque sylphe est-il son époux ?
Non, comme l'abeille elle est reine
D'un empire mystérieux ;
Vers son trône un de vous m'entraîne.
Sylphes légers, soyez mes dieux.

Yet her sportive, childish laughter
  Hides as bright a mother-wit,
As the dreams we follow after,
  And the marks we never hit.
Now a careless spark she flings,
  Now her tones the heart unseal;
You that lend her all your wings,
  Sylphs! to you alone I kneel.

Brilliant meteor, alas!
  She has vanished undescried.
Shall I once more see her pass?
  Or does some Sylph call her bride?
No! she rules, as rules the bee,
  Some mysterious commonweal;
To her hidden palace me
  Guide, O Sylphs, to whom I kneel!

À LA COMTESSE IDA.

Explication.

Si d'un enfant nous partageons la joie
Lorsque du jeu l'ardeur vibre en son corps,
S'il nous fait rajeunir lorsqu'il tournoie
Et saute, heureux comme un poulain sans mors ;

Ah ! combien plus je me sentais revivre
A vous voir belle, ardente de transport
Que soixante ans sont défendus de suivre,
A moins de vouloir recruter les morts ?

Alors que vous supposiez qu'insensible
Je dédaignais la chasse ce matin,
J'étais ravi, j'en fais l'aveu terrible,
Comme Actéon regardant Diane au bain.

Ainsi qu'on sent à voir tourner la danse
Battre le cœur et tressaillir le pied,
Je me trouvais dans un état de transe,
Devant le bonheur qui vous enivrait.

Vous auriez dit un courant mesmérique
Qui m'enlevait quarante ans bien sonnés,
Un adorable rêve magnétique
Dont le réveil s'exprime en bouts-rimés ?

MENTMORE, *February* 1882.

MA SAINTE AUX ROSES.

VIEIL ermite que je suis
Attendant la mort sans crainte,
Que tout serait plein d'ennuis,
Si je n'avais une Sainte !
J'ai tâché de m'incliner
Devant les Saintes qu'on prie ;
Je n'ai pu me prosterner
Qu'aux pieds d'une Sainte en vie.

Car celles dont les portraits,
Ornent tant de sanctuaires,
Ne sont que de vains reflets
Sauf aux yeux fervents des Pères.
Que me font ces tableaux de foi,
Œuvres d'artiste, de prêtre,
Quand elle, ma Sainte à moi,
Est l'œuvre du plus Grand Maître ?

Pauvre Abbé ! vos sombres toits
Rendant de l'Avé la phrase,
Ecrasent de tout leur poids
La sainte ardeur de l'extase ;
Tandis qu'aux prés, au bosquet,
Butinant les fleurs écloses,
J'en fais un charmant bouquet
Pour leur sœur, ma Sainte aux Roses.

L'Abbé voit à son reveil
Sa Madonne à peau de cire ;
Moi je rêve au teint vermeil
De ma Sainte, et son sourire ;
En songe, du Paradis
Il voit la cime lointaine,
Tandis que là, vis-à-vis,
Ma Sainte est ma Châtelaine.

STANCES À SIBELLE.

CELLE que j'aime est si belle
Qu'un voile d'or d'Immortelle
Semble flotter autour d'elle.
    Mais je suis mortel !
Et mon pauvre cœur se voile,
Elle est loin comme une étoile,
    Trônant dans le ciel ;

Mieux gardée droite et gauche
Que Danäe, dont l'approche
Défendait la vide poche
    D'un pauvre gardien,
Ebloui par la poussière
D'or du maître du tonnerre,
    Et s'en trouvant bien.

STANCES À SIBELLE.

Mon idéal, ma charmante,
Dont la beauté me tourmente
De bonheur et d'épouvante,—
    Mon doute, ma foi !
Même si j'avais les ailes
Des légères hirondelles,
    Atteindrais-je à toi ?

À MA GRACE DARLING.

Je cherchais dans le monde
    Ses bruits et ses oublis ;
Je voulais sous l'onde
    Noyer tous mes soucis.

La Folie enivrante
    Y guettait le plaisir ;
En vain la Corybante
    Amorçait mon désir.

Que le Seigneur exauce
    Mon besoin d'idéal,
Mais où l'on "fait la noce"
    N'est pas le Sangréal.

À MA GRACE DARLING.

O vous tous, pauvres hommes,
   Pour qui jouir est tout,
Vous mordez à des pommes
   Qui laissent le dégoût !

Comme, las de la fête,
   Je m'enfuyais bien loin,
Une angélique tête
   M'apparut dans un coin.

Je commencais à peine
   D'étudier ses traits,
Lorsqu'elle dit en reine
   "Suis moi ! je t'attendais."

Hors de la salle alerte,
   Mon cœur réalisait
Que, jouant à la perte,
   Le gros lot j'ai tiré.

Ballottée, en détresse
   Déjà sombrait ma barque,
Quand Laure, O sainte ivresse !
   Délivrait
                Son Pétrarque.

À LA PRINCESSE MARGOT.

Comment chanter ma Princesse,
    Dont l'aimable sœur
D'une semblable tendresse
    Fait bondir mon cœur?

Mais au nom de Saint Hercule
    Pourquoi prononcer,
Tant qu'elles comme pendule
    Me font balancer?

Je ne suis point girouette,
    Foi de papillon,
Quoique d'une escarpolette
    J'imite le bond.

À LA PRINCESSE MARGOT.

Entre vous, charmantes filles,
   Douteux mais dispos,
À ma goutte, à mes béquilles,
   J'ai donné campos.

Butinant comme l'abeille
   Jamais colibri
N'aura fortune pareille
   De voir, ébloui,

Un beau lis pur, une rose,
   Vrai parfum du ciel,
Chacune attendant qu'il ose
   Savourer son miel.

Vole donc, O balançoire
   Où le bonheur luit,
Avant que tombe la noire
   Mante de la nuit !

August 13, 1883.

À LAURE.

Je crains, ma blonde reine,
D'avoir perdu l'aubaine
   Dont vous me séduisiez ;
Et, toujours dans l'attente,
Je me sens sur la pente
   Des amis oubliés.

Mais quand, le soir, je rêve,
Quand Cupidon fait trêve,
   Et l'ombre du bonheur
Que votre image inspire
D'un innocent délire
   Fait tressaillir mon cœur ;

Alors je crois entendre,
Votre parler si tendre,
   Je vois briller vos yeux ;

À LAURE.

Votre douce main presse
La mienne avec ivresse,
   En écoutant mes vœux.

Hélas ! d'un si beau rêve
Que la durée est brève,
   Trajet de météore !
M'apprenant qu'à mon âge
L'amour devient mirage,—
   Tithone sans Aurore.

LONDON, *August* 1, 1883.

www.ingramcontent.com/pod-product-compliance
Lightning Source LLC
Chambersburg PA
CBHW021351230426
43666CB00006B/482